THE
JESUS
STORY

⟦ WILLIAM A. EMERSON, JR. ⟧

THE
JESUS
STORY

HARPER & ROW, PUBLISHERS

1817

NEW YORK   EVANSTON   SAN FRANCISCO   LONDON

FIRST EDITION

LIBRARY OF CONGRESS CATALOG CARD NUMBER: 70-148432

To Lucy

I salute Richard Gilbert for the audacious idea of the book and the temerity with which he stood by while it was being written. My gratitude to Barbara Catherine O'Dwyer who supplied unfailing tactical support and a superb instinct for the real character of the target. My deep appreciation to Calvin De Vries who shared his vision and his scholarship to an extraordinary degree. And I say thank you to my wife Lucy, who oversaw it all in a kindly, quiet and critical light which was my major illumination.

The Gospels of the New Testament do constitute a story. My purpose in this book is to retell "the Jesus Story" as it has struck me after reading many versions—old and recent—and after consulting a few reference and historical works. I have taken the liberty of integrating different versions of a certain narrative or story from time to time, and I have added a few elements of my own imagination. Grateful acknowledgment is made of permission by the Division of Christian Education of the National Council of the Churches of Christ to quote from *The Holy Bible, Revised Standard Version,* and permission by the American Bible Society to quote from *Good News for Modern Man: The New Testament in Today's English Version.*

THE
JESUS
STORY

[PROLOGUE]

JESUS OF NAZARETH is not some mythic figure from a lost civilization. If you see him conjured up out of heat waves from the magic of the Mediterranean cradle, you are over-looking good, solid information on his identity and back-ground. A Dun and Bradstreet on Jesus' family would have produced a conservative, uninteresting, low-risk profile of a substantial, lower middle-class family with half a dozen children. Jesus is the only one that turned out wrong—one brother became high priest in the Temple in Jerusalem some years after Jesus' execution.

You can look over a dark valley and see Palestine in the first century in a dazzling light. The century itself was quite extraordinary, enough like our own to make us uncomfortable. The Romans had things well in hand and were coming into their salad days. There was an accord of nations, a common market of sorts, satisfactory mails for the privileged, fine circuses and a very tolerable cuisine in urban areas. The judiciary was highly developed, plumbing was satisfactory, and banking was almost as complicated and as ominous as today. The Roman, with one of the most effective military machines of all times, was doing a splendid, if somewhat repressive, job of running the civilized world. And the little country of Palestine was just as colorful, feisty, difficult, hairy and uncommon as it is today.

Of course Palestine had been conquered by the Romans in 64 B.C., but this was no overwhelming fact. The indigestible little country had been previously conquered by the Babylonians, the Assyrians, twice by the Egyptians, by the Greeks, the kings of Antioch, the Persians. All were pungent, heavy-breathing captors. They seemed to have left the Jews with an enormous indisposition to change.

About the time Jesus came along, Rome was just getting accustomed to the unbelievable peculiarities of the Jews. The Jews would riot all week but they would not serve in the Roman legions because their religion forbade their fighting on the sabbath. They would not even look in a mirror on the sabbath because they might see a gray hair, and if they did, they might pull it out—that would be work. If a hen laid an egg on the sabbath, they were loath to eat it. They had two thousand incredible religious rules that took great scholarship even to remember, much less interpret. They couldn't eat with you, work out in the gym with you, or bow to your emperor. As a matter of fact, the Romans couldn't even take battle standards of their legions into Palestine because the Jews were driven to fanatical violence by the pagan symbols on the flags.

What could you do with a people like this? Nothing much, but the Romans kept their cool, made many compromises in the administration of the unforeseen; they kept the Jews under control, policed them and expected the worst. Then they got Jesus.

Now Jesus of Nazareth, living in the first century under Roman rule, was not a mild, manageable sort of person. He consorted with wild fire-eaters who got be-headed, like John the baptizer. At first everybody thought he was a bush-league rabble-rouser with a real gift of gab and a lot of magic tricks. Later events corrected that im-pression. He was a real incendiary influence. On his first trip back to preach in the meetinghouse in Nazareth, Jesus was almost lynched, which was not much of a welcome, even in those days. At first they thought he was a smart aleck, and then they condemned him for being blasphe-mous.

Jesus went on with a meteoric rise to become a super-star, and this brought him into deadly conflict with the Jewish establishment. This made what he said and what he did ten times as important. The Jews had a superb intelligence system and they knew what Jesus was up to all the time. They increasingly wanted his life. As for the Romans, they had a fine network of informers, but like all smart cops, they realized that Jesus was not their enemy. So they sat back and watched the action build.

There was some ebb and flow, but Jesus' course was highly charged and it was riven with spectacle. His life was almost entirely public, and he had no possessions, no property, no wife or children to draw him on or hold him back. He had the privacy of the wilderness and the road, but more and more it became impossible for him to go anywhere without being recognized. He drew vast crowds like the celebrities of this day, which both harassed and pleased him. He lived in the flux of the mob with the constant threat of being trampled to death or crushed, and in the suffocating heat, the dust and the dirt and the clamor. Yet Jesus was a very cool and composed person.

Paradoxically enough, we have an image of Jesus trapped in the stained-glass window down at the church. And in the filtered light we see a delicate, almost feminine figure with doe eyes and a reddish beard. This image is elusive, unreal; and, in translation, his voice is archaic. The icons of Christ have tempted too many brushes with pastel colors and too much gilt. Somehow the pungency has been sweetened and the fire banked. Jesus, the Pales-tinian Jew, hasn't traveled too well. The contemporary version is a faint print of the man who lived in the hills of Galilee two thousand years ago.

This "filtered" Jesus isn't the only one we have. In the aggregate there have likely been a whole troop of Jesuses—some marching as to war and some dawdling in the flowers with little children.

Each one has been minted by a different generation, is absolutely certified, and has the stamp of vintage. But, which is the real Jesus? Is it the sweet one that wants you to be a sunbeam? Is it the romanticized shepherd with one flaked-out lamb on his shoulder. Or maybe the hopeful teacher with the gelatinous eyes? Or could it be the guru scout leader with the Golden Rules? More likely, if you are from the Bible Belt, it is the vengeful one with the mouth like a sabre wound and the hot eyes. But you could be from the central city, and your Jesus would be the hippie Jesus, wearing a chenille bedspread and sandals, knocking the establishment and grooving along with all his brothers.

The obvious question is, who has taken all of this liberty with Jesus? Who had dye-cut him, popped him up, chipped him out, gnawed him out or clipped him out, and why did they do it? The answer is that they did it just to suit themselves. To find the sort of Jesus they could live with, be comfortable with. And this may be the reason that one always inherits an outmoded model of the Messiah, one that looks about as contemporary as an antimacassar. Faith has to make a mighty leap, a reck-less leap if we are going to accept as real a figure that has all of the characteristics of familiar unreality. It is just our luck now to have a spurious-looking composite put together by people who were terrified by love, but in love with goods, and this assemblage isn't appealing to a gen-eration that has a reverse instinct. People have reinforced what they thought he had to be by making him that.

' There is one abiding comfort, one Jesus we can cling to. There is one noncontroversial Jesus, utterly steady and secure. That is the baby Jesus. Nobody has ever produced a second version or a disturbing view of the baby Jesus. The shepherds and the wise men from the East regarded him together in perfect amity. At the time of Jesus' birth it was not quite this uncomplicated. Herod, the governor of Judea, was upset because the wise men and the astron-omers told him that they had studied the star when it came up in the east, and that the baby was to be the king of the Jews and they had come to worship him. Herod was a political animal, and he was not anxious to hear that this birth might be the fulfillment of prophecy that the Messiah would be born in Bethlehem, in Judea. Herod called together the scribes and the high priests to get it straight just where the baby was supposed to be born. The information upset them, and soon all of Jerusalem was talking about the birth of the Messiah.

At that point, Joseph and Mary were unaware that their baby Jesus was the cause of all of that high-level concern. The Roman Emperor Augustus had sent out an order that all of the citizens of the Empire were to register themselves for the census. To simplify the record, every-body was instructed to register in the home town of the family. Joseph, the carpenter, set out from Nazareth in Galilee to the town of Bethlehem in Judea where King David was born. Joseph was a descendant of David, as were many other Galileans, so they made up a friendly band and walked along the familiar route together. Mary, who was engaged to marry Joseph, went with him. Since she was well along in pregnancy, it is not unlikely that they felt there would be advantages to their child if he were born there.

Mary was startled when she found out she was going to be a mother, and Joseph was dismayed when he found out that his betrothed was going to have a child, for they had not had sexual relations. But just as Joseph in his kind and wise way was planning to marry Mary and then divorce her quietly to avoid any public scandal, he had a dream. An angel appeared to Joseph and told him not to be afraid to take Mary as his wife, that the Holy Spirit was the father of the child. Joseph accepted this, and they found themselves in Bethlehem when the time came for the baby to be born.

Very little is known about the birth of Jesus. The great influx of people had filled all of the rooms in the inn, and Mary had her baby in a stable that Joseph had fixed up for her. After the baby was born, Mary wrapped him in cloths and laid him gently on fresh straw in a manger.

Agents of Herod the king were checking out the neighborhood to see if they could locate the child of prophecy. But, they were not astronomers, and they may well have overlooked Mary and Joseph and Jesus because they were not registered in the inn. Joseph was confronted by an angel in a dream. "Get up, take the child and his mother and run away to Egypt," the angel said, "and stay there until I tell you to leave. Herod will be looking for the child to kill him." Joseph left during the night for Egypt, and he stayed there with his family until Herod died.

When Herod found out that he had been tricked, he was enraged. He gave an order to his soldiers to kill all of the boys in Bethlehem and its neighborhood who were two years old and younger. Though Jesus escaped, many children were killed.

In the frantic night flight, Joseph took Jesus and Mary down the desolate desert road to Egypt that is known as the Sinai Gate; it goes into the southern Negeb through the Kadesh-barnea region. Joseph was a provident, hardy man and his talent for survival foreshadowed the exploits of his tough-minded son who got to know the wilderness areas of Palestine like the back of his hand during the many months that he was on the road.

After Herod died, an angel came to Joseph in a dream and told him to get his family back to Israel. Joseph decided to go back to Galilee because he knew that Herod's son Archelaus had succeeded his father as King of Judea. They went back to Nazareth, and Jesus grew up there. His brothers and sisters were born there, and the household was devout and conservative. Galilee as a region was full of fall-away Jews, but Joseph and Mary stuck to the old-time religion until long after Jesus was gone.

Jesus grew up in the midst of a people who, historically, had confounded the world. They had confounded the Greeks, they confounded the Romans, and the records of their soul-searching and agonizing self-appraisal suggests that they confounded themselves. Their psychic lives were thickly furred and phantasmagoric; their social and religious lives were honeycombs of ritual and rule, but most of them were profoundly religious. Their public lives were full of violence, intrigue and fanaticism. Jesus came from these ferocious, idiosyncratic people, and he was to spend his public life contesting with them. By maintaining their separateness, the Jews had preserved their identity through exile and dispersal and occupation. Of all of their possessions, the most precious and the best protected was their religion. Jesus set about giving it away.

⟦ STARDOM ⟧

IT WAS the greatest evangelistical road show of all time. Everybody came. People on the side of the road to beg, to die or just to watch the world go by all got in the act. Blind beggars, lepers, pickpockets and magicians, tumblers and acrobats, hustling prostitutes, venders of food aromatic and vile, idle soldiers, slaves in yokes and chains, and freckle-bellied folks of every color clotted the way. Rubes and scholars and lesser messiahs and Zealots, along with spies from the Pharisees, jostled the usual thick gruel of village and townspeople under the almond trees for a view of Jesus, and cupped their ears to hear that clear pen-etrating voice piercing the glittering air as the sun caught dust particles in the ebbing heat of the afternoon.

The whole thing had the air of a circus with its freaks and animals and the endless variety of bizarre spectacle that Mediterranean humanity affords. Jesus was a poet and a one-man band. Barnstorming in the open country wasn't much like preaching in a hushed temple or church. Jesus was on the meetinghouse circuit too. He had an inside-outside convertible act that he took to every crossroad, changing the pace and the pitch at a moment's notice. He talked in the synagogues of myriad little towns of Galilee and Judea. And there he clashed with the religious leaders and the scholars; he parried the cunning questions of the informers; he brought good news to the curious; and he scratched questions that would not heal across the consciousness of the incurious.

Jesus' itinerary stretched north to Caesarea Philippi, east into the Ten Towns of the Decapolis, and west into Phoenicia as well as through the outback of Samaria where Jews were not comfortable traveling. But his mission centered around the Sea of Galilee and a wide swath of towns on the northern and western shores of the Dead Sea. The muddy, serpentine Jordan River which connects these two areas is only two hundred miles long. Jesus and his companions covered thousands of miles on foot, however, in a series of walking tours that took them over some wild and forbidding terrain.

The experience of delivering the message face to face had an overwhelming effect on him. The sensorial impact of the whole land underfoot was compounded by the violent contrasts of weather and topography that are typical of Palestine. On a single trip Jesus might venture from the cold, bare mountainsides of Galilee to the subtropical Jordan valley, and from there to the scorching desert near Jericho. Temperatures rose to 120° F. at midday across stretches that Jesus frequently traveled. This land was so inhospitable under the full sun that sheep were sometimes grazed at night and human beings kept to the shade to stay alive. Yet the land of pitiless desert also offered prodigal fertility in the watered areas where figs, almonds, luscious grapes and incomparable olives grew.

Across this landscape moved an unlikely mixture of wild animals. When Jesus was afoot, lions and leopards, once abundant, were disappearing, but there were bear in the mountains, hyenas in the foothills, and there was a plentiful supply of jackals and foxes, and rabbits and other small critters. Jesus walked everywhere he went, in touch with birds and beasts, with trees and wild flowers, with the shape and feel of the country. It must have been a time of great learning as well as a time of teaching.

The physical exertion of walking over the rugged, broken landscape would have been a perfect balance for the exhausting intellectual confrontations in the meeting-houses. Hard exercise helped dissolve the kinks in Jesus' mind, and periods of comparative privacy along the way gave him time to ruminate over his intent. Obviously, his was a complex life, rich and feverish and at the same time full of strain and perplexity. He had a lot to ponder.

To understand how his work might have affected him, we need only consider ourselves. We are not that distant from the first century. Jesus stood at the end of almost two millennia of civilized life. He was literate. He had a grasp of the composition of the civilized world of his time. All that he knew and experienced came together into some sort of coherent mosaic. Curiously, a general feeling of malaise, which we can discern today, hung over the first century, too. Most of us do not share the same sense of onrushing personal crisis that steadily grew in Jesus' consciousness, but we recognize personal uneasiness and parlous times.

Jesus was not only literate in Aramaic and Hebrew, but he also certainly knew some Greek and Latin. There was compulsory education in Palestine for all male Jewish children, at least until the age of fifteen, and although the curriculum was entirely religious it would have in- volved his learning to read and write with facility in his own tongue and in Hebrew. Business Greek was the uni- versal language of his time and he would have been ex- posed to it often, especially when he visited towns that had been Hellenized. Most Jews were comfortable with Greek; in one Jewish graveyard of his period 80 percent of the inscriptions of the stones were Greek.

He could not have avoided regular contact with the governing Romans with whom he conversed either in Latin or in Greek. As a matter of fact, he seemed to talk to everyone wherever he went. You could think of his speeches as being something like a Town Hall lecture series. Jesus was booked as a learned teacher but his audience got more than they bargained for. There was more controversy than is compatible with good business. He was more than stimulating, he was incendiary. With humor and with ferocity, he attacked his society for its materialism and its inhumanity, and he assailed his coun- trymen as irresponsible stewards of their religion and neglectors of the spiritual need of their brothers. He told simple but punishing stories about people who didn't want to get involved. And he made it clear that an obsession with wealth or legalism was idolatry. It is powerfully evident from reading again and again what he said that the forces and temptations which demean and stain the human spirit have been the same in the first and twentieth centuries.

The tyranny of the stock market, pensions, social conformity—we accept all of that in a mythic wrong-way flight to security. The reality of being free, however, requires being able to accept the frightening implications of what we yearn for. Jesus talked incessantly about putting aside material things and even members of one's family; what he was getting at was a point of view, an insight into the nature of false servitude, a vision of liberation. The smothering acquisitiveness of his time was the jailer of souls just as it is today. When he went after this, Jesus went after all privilege, all position, all ambition; he went for the jugular of the establishment. There is no chance of reconciliation once this intent is recognized.

Any accurate view of Jesus has got to be affected by the great physical exertion in his life. He was always in action. When he was in repose it was late at night, a day's work over, the crowd finally disposed of. The fire of energy shone around him, and he was still awake when his tough fishermen friends had dozed off. We have a stereotyped portrait of the minister of Christ as being a little pale and puffy. Jesus would have scared such a minister out of his pulpit. He was lean, weathered, sinewy, like a paratrooper after a long campaign. His life was more spartan and he probably got more exercise than the average soldier, for he lived behind the lines like a guerrilla or a partisan of the underground. It was traveling light—vigilant, tireless, always moving on, surviving on that delicate balance between being a fugitive and being a public figure.

What was Jesus actually doing? Well, he was traveling and working and organizing all the time. He was pushing his luck like a union organizer in the cotton mills in the 20's, or like a civil rights worker in Mississippi in the 50's. He was living on the edge. Today he'd live under the kind of suspense a Black Panther or a Weatherman knows, aware that his cause has passionate support, aware that opposition is going to build ten times as fast as the strength of the cause. Jesus knew as surely as Martin Luther King knew that he was going to get it, and he just didn't have the scapegrace chance of a Barabbas or a Jesse James. Jesus had to make that last run to Jerusalem, but shrewd Jesse declined the last gambit and lived to a ripe and contented old age. Jesus was not finally trapped by the kind of exposure he had. He was not unlucky—he was the victim of a plot. The teacher himself wove the plot bit by bit, and he gradually came to foresee the type of victim he would be.

Jesus' work got under way when he left Nazareth in the hills of Galilee one morning. He had made other trips across Palestine, and had actually been born in Bethlehem when the family journeyed down to register in the census. This one was a great leavetaking. It was the fateful beginning of a goal that would entirely possess him and from which he would never turn back. It was a hard walk from Galilee to Judea, but he did not view that as a problem. An irresistible compulsion prompted the trip. He was leaving to find John, a cousin on his mother's side, who had suddenly burst into national prominence as a fireball wilderness preacher in Judea near Jerusalem.

Traveling through Palestine as a first-century Jew would have been like a Southerner traveling from Charleston to Savannah before the Civil War. Palestine was smaller than the American South, but the populations were of comparable size—about five million—and family connections made each a network of friends and relations. You, or somebody you knew, knew somebody of consequence everywhere you went. There was a turnover population of Romans and slaves and visiting businessmen, but a thirty-year-old Jew could find himself at home anywhere in Palestine.

Galilee was the most populous part of Palestine, bustling and prosperous. Some of the landscape, nevertheless, was wizard and intricate, and other parts wild and forbidding, but firsthand acquaintance and folk memory from his nomadic forebears gave Jesus an easy grasp of all of it. As Jesus crossed the roads and trails of the foothills which lead across the territory to the Dead Sea, he was constantly recognizing people that he knew—friends going on visits to nearby towns, slaves running errands, associates of his tradesman father. Roman soldiers were always in evidence along the way. They were from the four regular legions stationed in Palestine or from special legions that were moved in and out depending on the disposition of the times. Horses from elements of the cavalry and beasts from the camel corps attached to each legion left their signs along the roads and could be seen tethered near the garrisons scattered along the major routes. The presence of the Romans, who enforced law and order, made life comparatively safe along the most traveled parts of Jesus' route, but there is no reason to think he was serene.

The suspense that comes to all men when they take the first step toward a mysterious and fateful commitment held Jesus' mind and turned his thoughts inward. He spoke, greeted acquaintances casually, but as he traveled the distance to the lower Jordan he was traveling a greater distance in his mind. The inner trip, doubtlessly, was the more engrossing one, and it didn't leave a lot of attention for social pleasantries. To get to the desert country of northern Judea, Jesus had to walk down from the Galilean hills to the Valley of Jezreel; for a time the trail led down a spine of sharp ridges without vegetation. The rough, corrugated terrain was endlessly serrated into conical hills and plunging valleys, so the demands of his path quieted the trace of dread in Jesus' thoughts, a temp-orary luxury that diminished as he got closer to Jericho and the wilderness beyond—north of the Dead Sea.

More and more people along the way were talking about his cousin John, John the baptizer as he was begin-ning to be called. According to his billing John was a figure who had appeared at a divinely appointed time. The spontaneous response to his prophecy seemed to justify the billing. Throngs of people poured out of Jerus-alem to listen and to be immersed in the Jordan. The scene was one of great commotion with the shouting of this wild man battering the complacency of anyone who heard his preaching. His message contained the critical news people have sought in every historical age: the world was coming to an end. John was crying in the wilderness that the Kingdom was at hand, and he preached salvation through repentance and ritual immersion in the water of the Jordan. The only alternative he held out to the evil was that they would be destroyed by unquenchable fire.

Crowds were thunderstruck by him. Sophisticated gentry were as stunned by him as were the commoners. Pharisees, the religious elite, offered themselves for baptism. John flayed them with abuse and called them snakes, and he mocked them for fleeing the terrible wrath that was to come. This relentless man was so heedless of protecting himself that he had attacked and embarrassed Herod, the tetrarch of Galilee—the Jewish kingfish. Once John had riveted the national attention he confounded the crowds by denying that he himself was even as much as a prophet. There was, he said, a man who would be coming along whose shoes John was not worthy to untie, and that man would baptize not with water but with the Holy Spirit and fire.

Jesus turned a bend in the river and finally came upon John, a fierce-looking apparition dressed in a camel's hair robe with a leather thong around his waist. His presence was as bright as flame. The crowd pressed in upon John, but Jesus caught his attention. There was hesitation. John earnestly questioned the propriety of his baptizing Jesus, and Jesus reassured him, and it was done.

When Jesus came out of the water, everything had changed. Standing there together, both men were transformed by an awareness that inexorable powers were working through them to arrange a destiny. And then Jesus felt overwhelmed by the presence and approval of God. In his revelation he saw the heavens open and the Spirit come down on him. He was suffused with a voice that said, "You are my own dear son. I am well pleased with you."

A blistering day on the turgid, syrupy Jordan was the break-off point between the unfathomable selection and preparation of Jesus, and the relentless way he lived his ministry. If it was hazy and soft when Jesus was born at Bethlehem, now the mist had burnt off and the air was agate hard. John was the dynamite cap that set Jesus off. Along the Jordan and in the wilderness John had lived on locusts and honey from wild bees, and he had suffered visions of a new life. So that his mind might burn with revelation in a totally uncontaminated way, he had never even had a drink of wine. He isolated himself in an inhospitable expanse of wilderness that got into the mind and left it windswept, bleak, clear. In that unclut-tered space John could build a new kind of religion and pass it on. He was a torrential life force, a waterfall with no boulders, no sandbars.

John swept away all the easy assurances about salva-tion and substituted a terrifying gospel. "You snakes," he called the eager and anxious elite waiting to be baptized. Then he lambasted them for assuming they had gained any special dispensation because they were descendants of Abraham. Just as Isaiah had predicted, one had come to prepare the way. To make the path straight. To bring the hills and mountains low. John.

Jesus got the prototype of his work from John. At the beginning John provided not only the ignition but also a cadre of followers to Jesus. These men stayed with

Jesus until the end. The words of John were still in the desert air when Jesus walked away from his baptism. Soon he would begin his own work with similar phrases: "Turn away from your sins! The kingdom of heaven is at hand."

Immediately after his baptism Jesus walked out of the waters of the Jordan into the wild desert that is so near you can see the edges of it from the bank of the Jordan. It was the closest refuge. Jesus was filled with an over-powering sense of the presence of God, and the emptiness of the desert helped him contain within himself the ex-ploding sense of the holy visitation. This was one of three times in Jesus' life that he felt himself literally connected to God. In the first of the forty days he spent fasting in the desert he crossed a Rubicon that separated him from all the comforts and assurances and expectations he had had as Jesus, son of Joseph and Mary, brother of James, Joseph, Simon and Judas and a number of sisters.

If the desert was endless and baleful, with no landmarks that you could depend on, the interior landscape of Jesus' mind was a match for it. There were no psychic land-marks either, only an unremitting sense of being at a be-ginning. He was possessed by the realization that he had been separated out for a destiny he did not completely understand. As he searched the caves of his own mind he began to discern the way but he could not tell exactly where it would lead. If God had connected with him, that was as much as he could understand in the loneliness of the desert in one moment. One thing was clear. He was still a man. A man with a great power of slow revelation working inside him.

As vulnerable as every human being, Jesus was menaced

by wild animals, but they smelled no fear in him and stood off. Satan was not so easily put off. He spoke with tremendous authority; it was as though he had private information on the unbearable tension Jesus felt between the power settling in him and the pains of hunger that demanded some kind of relief and deliverance. If Jesus really had the power he tremulously felt he had, could he make it work for himself? This explosive temptation took the form of the Devil. It was irresistible. If Jesus could in fact turn stones into bread, he could ease his ravenous hunger. And if he couldn't, then he could let go of the terrifying possibilities he had been imagining and become an ordinary man again. Yet had not the prophets written, "Man shall not live by bread alone, but by every word that proceeds from the mouth of God." Slowly he got control of his hunger.

Then the Devil took over Jesus' consciousness and transported him to the highest point of the Temple in Jerusalem. Looking down from the dizzying height, Jesus felt the deadly ecstasy that you feel when you lean far out over the edge of a great building. It was an extraordi- nary height for the spirit as well as the eye, for the Jerusalem Temple was the holiest of shrines. If Jesus had thrown himself from the peak of the Temple and plum- meted toward the paving stones, to be caught at the last moment by a net of angels, he could have overcome the leaders of Jerusalem. There they were in the court- yard below and in the Temple. If these were the people he was going to be pitted against, and his whole intuition told him they were, why not blitz them from the begin- ning? Leaning out in the bright air with the wind whistling, Jesus knew the temptation to tempt God, and he closed his mind to it. But there was another temptation of an opposite and more cunning sort, a prize many hearts cannot decline. The Devil, who is of course the finest hard-sell artist of all time when he puts his mind to it, presented this last deal very carefully. He took Jesus to the very top of a cloudless sky, and said, "Look at that!"

All the kingdoms curved away below him. The sum total accomplishments of man in all his appetites and ambitions and dreams were there. All the things of the earth man had stored up were laid out like a glittering tapestry. The Devil gave it time to soak in, and then he made his proposition. "The power and glory of all of this can be yours," he said. "You can be king. You can take all the kingdoms of the earth right now, with no probation time. Say yes now. All you have to do is kneel down and worship me, and it will be yours."

In one moment he could be the ultimate man. It was within his grasp if he said yes. How could he tell what was in store for him if he followed the lead of his ecstatic baptism? There were two masters, but this one had made the clearer pitch. Too clear. The Devil had pressed too hard; he had overplayed his hand. If this was the bonus for going against God, what could be the consequence of going with God? The rapture Jesus still held from the baptism triumphed. There he stood in the wilderness which was inside and outside of him, and he stood there as a man full of passion and soul. He could not let go of what he could not see to take what he could see. Offered the world, he could give it up. The Devil understood the implication of this and retired from the field.

The ordeal of temptation left Jesus absolutely spent. Then out of his exhausture a great exhilaration came and he was enveloped by an all-encompassing wave of peace and serenity. Jesus knew it was time to leave the desert, and since there was nothing to pack and no one to check out with, he was on his way. The wind whipped sand over his footprints and the experience was behind him.

Almost immediately he became aware of the distress on the faces of people milling about on the bank of the Jordan. John the baptizer had been arrested and imprisoned. Those who had walked long distances to hear him speak found it hard to accept the cruelty and finality of the arrest. The skeptical ones were the most despairing of all because now that they could not hear him they were certain that they would have been saved by believing John. The broadcast of John's arrest was a shock to Jesus and, at the same time, a signal. His cousin was gone; there was no reason for him to remain in Judea.

Jesus took stock of himself and for the first time since he had left Nazareth he began to make plans for the future. John had been a one-man spectacular. Now he was gone and the atmosphere of the bare and beaten-down fan-shaped bank of the Jordan where he had held his revival meetings was trashy and desolate, Woodstock the morning after. The traces left of the smoldering camp meetings were like the ashes of a vanished fire. The disciples of John were still there, however, hopelessly trying to greet new arrivals and answer questions of the troubled who remained. Jesus fell in with this group. John had talked about him; some had seen Jesus' baptism; all saw the mark of the prophet on Jesus.

Of course Jesus was accepted and a place made for him at the fires where meals were being prepared. Grief was well fed. The training days of locusts and wild honey were over, and sumptuous meals of lamb and fowl with bread, cheese, dates, ample rich olive oil, figs and wine were some solace to the rear guard who were breaking camp. Provisions were turned over in mute sympathy by those of means who had been baptized or unsettled by John. Just as friends bake cakes and cook chickens today to nourish the spirit of people in sorrow, so did the Jews. They were well practiced in the language of adversity. Jesus quickly regained his strength. He was hungry for companionship, and his conversations around the fires at night brought him very close to Andrew, Simon Peter's brother. There was instant recognition between them.

Andrew had been standing with John the baptizer when Jesus first saw him. After Jesus' baptism, Andrew had brought his brother Simon Peter to meet him. The two brothers swiftly moved into the circle of John's aware- ness that Jesus' baptism was a momentous occasion, and that Jesus somehow was an apocalyptic event in the life and purpose of John. The reunion of the three crystal- lized the feeling in each that they should be moving on, and then it was inevitable that they should go back to their home region, Galilee, together.

Andrew and Peter had been fishermen before they encountered John. Both had made their living on that cur- ious, treacherous, shallow body of water, the Sea of Gali- lee. It was rich in natural food and abounded with fish, but it was a nasty, quick-tempered bit of water that drew storms out of the Mediterranean Sea and magnified them.

Surviving on it made men crotchety, weather-wise and, some said, mercurial. Anyway, its fishermen were men whose instincts for disaster were finely whetted. Storms came up quickly across the uplands of Galilee and sucked furiously down into the basin of the sea, roiling the water into murderous waves. Men who live in balance with the elements develop a quick response to nature. One could see the imprint in Peter and Andrew.

They were overawed by John. He was simple, elemental. The ferocity of the man struck admiration in them, and his fearlessness won their total allegiance. He could smell the sky and call the weather, just as they could; he could sense where water lay in the dry desert as surely as they could navigate through black night or deep fog to land. It was the brotherhood of those skilled in reading nature. This life made the indulgences, the luxuries, the mannerisms of the city people somehow contemptible, and their customs and rituals unnecessary and absurd. When John was arrested they were thunderstruck. They had not been able to defend John, and without him, Andrew and Peter were like abandoned children.

The two fishermen could not in any way compare Jesus to John. Jesus had not grown up in the desert. He was a Nazarene. Jesus' background in Joseph's substantial working-class home had no reality for them. Jesus had come alive for them through the mystical experience in the river with John. John had said he was not worthy to untie Jesus' sandals. He had actually tried to refuse to baptize Jesus; they were puzzled about that. But the simple matter of it was that once they were with Jesus and ready to set out for Galilee they felt more comfort-

able and secure about everything. The long walk back
to Galilee gave the three time to talk about John, but the
route was not without its distractions. It was not sensible
to follow the serpentine Jordan which curved endlessly
in switchback s's through dense jungle. So they walked
out the Jericho Road to the ancient route that led up
the Jordan rift from Jericho to the Sea of Galilee and
then west to Accho on the Mediterranean. The first
segment of the trail cut across tangled thickets watered by
the Jordan. In the evening Jesus and his companions
could hear the snapping of the jaws of crocodiles and the
occasional cries of wild animals in the tamarisk groves
along the riverbanks. After they had made camp the first
night the roar of a young lion came from the black woods
in the bottom land to the east of the trail; it cleared
everybody's mind of the problems they had discussed
during the day.

By unspoken consent, Jesus, Andrew and Peter had
agreed not to take the main highway, or the Water-
Parting route as it was called, that led north through
the main towns of Palestine. Since it connected Hebron,
Bethlehem, Jerusalem, Gibeah, and curved on up through
Mizpah, Shiloh and Shechem to Megiddo, that route
would be crawling with traffic—soldiers relieving con-
tingents stationed in Jersualem and traders working the
inland markets. The three were still consumed with the
matter of trying to fathom what lay ahead in their lives.
The wild hawk soaring over the steep slopes to the west
of the trail was no more lonely and searching than the
minds of these men as they walked north. The attachment
of Andrew and Peter to Jesus became very powerful as

they listened to him talk about John. A new alliance began
to form.

The walk home was hardly long enough for the two
fishermen to come to any final conclusions. They felt a
strong desire to get back to their boats and nets after
the disaster of John's arrest, but the revelation that had
turned their lives upside down was open ended. The three
separated. Before Jesus left the fishermen near the shore
north of Tiberias they talked quietly about Jesus' conviction that John's message could not be locked up even
though he was in prison. "The Kingdom is at hand," he
said, "the people must repent and be born anew or God
will destroy them with unquenchable fire. We must preach
the news." As he walked off toward Capernaum he
called after them, "When I am ready, I will come and
get you."

Jesus reached Capernaum the next morning after spend-
ing the night with old friends along the familiar way.
Immediately he began speaking in the meetinghouses. The
great energies that had been bottled up in the desert and
on the soul-searching walk back to Galilee poured out. The
way seemed cleared and clearer. Jesus was convinced
that he should devote himself to preaching repentance
with all the urgency he could muster. If he was still perplexed about his ultimate destiny the day was sufficient to
itself. It was like plunging into ice water, this new work.
His passion to speak out was satisfied, but there was one
ordeal he had to face right away.

Galilee was home, but Nazareth was hometown, and
Jesus had a knot in his stomach when he thought about
preaching there. Religious news in Palestine had the

currency of political news on the New York-Washington axis; it moved like lightning. Rumors about Jesus were linked to the reports of the arrest of John. There were hazy accounts of Jesus' baptism and contradictory reports about what John and Jesus had said there. In a way Jesus had already become a minor-league prophet, and reports of his preaching in the meetinghouses preceded him to Nazareth. There was even talk that he had performed magic and miraculous healings. The curiosity was tempered with some incredulity toward reports of what he had said.

Jesus' advance billing made his family extremely uneasy. His message that the Kingdom was at hand made the Jews uptight because, however casual some of the populace might seem to be about their religion, they had been conditioned for more than a thousand years to expect the unexpected. There was a hallowed tradition of prophecy and everybody was susceptible to it, but there were not so many prophets that you expected the son of the family next door to be one.

Then, suddenly, Jesus was actually in Nazareth. The sabbath came, bringing a peak of uneasiness to his family, and Jesus went to the synagogue as he customarily did. It was a hard game to play before the hometown folks, but Jesus didn't choke up. He stood up to read the scripture given to him which, not wholly accidentally, was the Book of Isaiah. If it was a trap there was no way to step around it. Jesus had the wit and courage to face the question of who he was and what he had in mind. So he read: "The Spirit of the Lord is upon me, because he has anointed me to preach good news to the poor. He has

sent me to proclaim release to the captives and recovery
of sight to the blind, to set at liberty those who are oppressed. . . ."

He had the attention of the house and he made the
most of it. Jesus told them that this revered bit of scripture had been fulfilled before their very eyes. They began
to take the measure of him as he talked, but it was a slow
measure. At first they praised the hometown boy; how
gracefully he put everything. Jesus knew that he had a
deadly serious role to play, that he couldn't be one sort
of person in Capernaum and another in Nazareth. There
was no way to turn back. He went ahead. He could hear
some of his listeners discussing all this fuss being made
over Joseph's son. What had he done in Capernaum that
had started the rumors? Why didn't he do his tricks?
Everybody could then judge for himself whether Jesus
was a magician. Jesus could smell the curiosity and the
underlying hostility.

"You are thinking," he said, " 'Physician, heal yourself—do in your own hometown what you did in Capernaum.' " Then he put the seal on what they were thinking.
"I'm here to tell you that no prophet is acceptable in
his own country." He recounted the time that Elijah had
overlooked all the widows in his own land during a great
famine, and had gone to Zarephath in Sidon to single
her out for special help; and how Naaman the Syrian
general, who was a bad-tempered, arrogant man at that,
had been cured of leprosy by Elisha when Israel was full
of lepers. The listeners at the synagogue rose as one man,
indignant and ready for action. He thought he was too
good for them.

They threw Jesus out of the city, and then, as an after-thought, pushed him to the top of a hill on which the city was built so that they could throw him off the edge. Yet there was a hesitance about actually overpowering him, and he walked away through the crowd. He left behind a humiliated, confused family. He had become a new sort of holy man which was more than a simple family could contend with.

Jesus left Nazareth with relief and with insight into his relationship to his family and his home. This violent departure was the last psychological break. Jesus always stayed in touch with his family after the incident in Nazareth and dropped in on relatives when he was teaching nearby, but now he was completely independent of them. It was as if people everywhere became his family. It was not possible to take kinfolk along on the life that was taking shape for him. People could not be indifferent to the strong message he was preaching; they were going to be hot or cold.

Looking back on the wedding at Cana, which had taken place just a few days before the debacle at Nazareth, Jesus saw his mother in a different light. There had been so many relatives and friends there that the wine gave out to the confoundment of the caterer and the despair of the few guests aware of the problem. It had been just like his mother to defer the dilemma to him. She said, "They have no wine." "I know, I know," he said with instant irritation. "What would you have me do, woman?" He knew perfectly well what any mother would have her son do in a situation like that if she could. And she would love to have everyone witness it.

Mary rounded up the servants and pointed to her son and said, "Do whatever he tells you." His mother knew of the powers her son reputedly had.

Jesus was not anxious to get into catering; it was certainly not a time to do frivolous miracles on the banquet circuit. What could he do? Jesus ordered the servants to fill six available stone jars with water. Then hurriedly, almost secretly, he turned the water into wine. He had a servant take some to the head caterer who was amazed at the quality and assumed the host had just broken out a reserve store. "Most people serve the good wine first, and when the guests are drunk they serve the poor wine," he said in honest surprise. The guests went joyously about their business, unaware that a near catastrophe and a miracle had taken place.

Jesus' mother knew, of course, and she had not conceived that he could fail in Nazareth. Mary had expected him to be triumphant, to do the family proud. He had the wonderful power. Certainly he would convince the skeptics in his hometown. Jesus began to see the irony of his role. He began to suspect that he would not satisfy all who wanted to believe in him.

Glad to have Nazareth behind him, Jesus felt the satisfaction of being free to do his work as he saw it. He walked along the shore of the Sea of Galilee looking for Andrew and Peter. There were many fishing boats beached that day, and Jesus could tell by the lack of activity that it had not been a good day. By that hour they should have been well out in the long, narrow sea maneuvering their nets. He saw the boats he was looking for; the owners and hired hands were in the shallow water washing the nets. Jesus climbed into Peter's boat, and Andrew, who was working nearby on a net, started over. Peter waved a greeting, finished speaking with a friend, and joined Jesus. There was a warm exchange of welcome and recollection, and then Jesus asked Peter to push his boat into the water and away from the shore a little so that he could speak to the families and acquaintances of the fishermen who had come to the shore to see how the catch had been.

He spoke with authority and the people on the beach listened carefully, and others came from nearby fields. He said they could not see the approaching kingdom of God unless they were reborn by accepting baptism after repentance. Simon Peter and Andrew saw the power he had with crowds. Suddenly he had finished. Jesus didn't like long speeches or prayers and he practiced what he liked, so what he said was brief, even elliptical. Turning to his friends, he said, "Put the boat out into deep water, and you and your partners can let your nets down for a catch." They shrugged their shoulders. Peter said, "We worked hard all night and caught nothing. They are just not feeding. But, if you say so." They dropped the nets.

The nets filled so that Andrew and Peter had to strain, and still the nets almost gave way. They shouted to their partners and a second boat joined them, with all the fisher-men struggling with the enormous catch. The nets were pulled in but it appeared for a time that the boats them-selves might sink under the weight of the catch. They got the situation in hand and then looked at what had hap-pened. Peter threw himself down in front of Jesus, setting his knees in a mound of slippery fish, and said with the

force of sudden revelation, "Go away from me, Lord, for
I am a sinful man!" The miracle of the catch overwhelmed
all the fishermen who were aware of what had occurred,
particularly James and John, Simon Peter's partners, who
were sons of a man named Zebedee. Jesus had talked to
the sailors in a language they could understand, and he
had worked a miracle within the reality that they completely understood. His communication was complete,
and they were dismayed. So Jesus comforted them.

"Don't be afraid," he told them. "From now on you
will be catching men." The boats were pulled up on the
beach and abandoned. Jesus had not only been reunited
with Peter and Andrew but had swept James and John
into his net. The five of them set off in high spirits, bound
together now by common experiences of the ordinary
and the miraculous. Jesus led the group to Capernaum
where he had taken up temporary residence. On the
sabbath he went again to the meetinghouse and spoke.
His new companions saw that the crowd was deeply impressed with Jesus' words. His thoughts pierced the minds
of followers and strangers alike in electrifying encounters.
It was this living experience in meetinghouse after meetinghouse, town after town, which changed the followers
as human beings and was an apprenticeship for everything
that lay ahead.

Jesus' life on the road was a process of educating and con-
ditioning his disciples. These men were gradually re-created
to represent an understanding of the good news he talked
about. When he succeeded they became embodiments of
his gospel, and when he failed, a long shot for the
future had fallen short. But he was willing to gamble.

He took the audacious risk that his views would live in these men and pass living from them to others in a way that no written message or code ever could.

It is conceivable that Jesus personally spoke to as many as half of the five million Jews who lived in Palestine in his time. He made permanent changes in the people he spoke to—in a blinding flash he could reveal a whole new life, and more. He was not just inspiring or encouraging, he had a powerful close. Jesus gave his prescription for salvation, and he celebrated the rescue of a single soul as if the world had been saved. His converts were profoundly changed because they had a new concept of God and a new concept of self and a new concept of their fellow men—this is a cluster of beliefs that could literally make a new person. But there was another dimension that made his work so moving and so effective. In addition to chang- ing people's beliefs, he also changed their bodies. And he cured their minds.

During his first days in Capernaum after the enlist- ment of Peter and Andrew, and James and John, Jesus was challenged by a man in the meetinghouse who had an evil demon in him. He screamed at Jesus, "What do you want with us, Jesus of Nazareth? Are you here to destroy us? I know who you are: you are God's holy messenger." The madman understood Jesus' power, and his madness resisted Jesus as a natural enemy. Jesus told the demon to shut up. "Be quiet and come out of the man." The demon threw the man down in front of them all, and went out without doing the man harm. Jesus' response to the demonic revealed a good deal about his courage and composure. As was his wont with demons and evil spirits Jesus took on the challenge directly. It is likely that a first-century Palestinian was more responsive to madness than to any other ailment. Jesus felt that the mad had first priority, because they had no chance to accept him until they had been given possession of themselves.

He was not a prototype of the modern medical missionary, dispensing nostrums and working psychiatric cures. In our time this is a commonplace pursuit of an ordinary ideal. In the first century, however, people were extremely calloused toward human suffering. The governing Romans had almost unrivaled capacity for casual cruelty and a positive talent for adapting, and improving on, methods of torture encountered in their eastern empire. Crucifixion was fairly humdrum, except to the victim, and on one historic occasion the Romans crucified two thousand men at one time. They stopped only when they ran out of wood for more crosses. In this sort of culture, a healing ministry which showed passionate concern for the sufferer must have seemed like lunacy.

Inevitably this man with a curious taste for curing people and extracting demons was pursued by a horde of lepers, nuts, paralytics, the deaf, dumb and blind, and those possessed of all manner of fits and contagious diseases of every degree of virulency. You could think of these socially undesirable people as the seasoning of the larger mass who came simply to satisfy curiosity or to flee damnation. It was in his masterly management of this volatile tissue of humanity that Jesus expressed his genius for recording the living word ready for transmission down through the generations.

The main engagements in Jesus' travels were the meetinghouses, but his revival circuit embraced the watering stops, marketplaces, garrison towns and resorts. His fame as a healer spread into Samaria and from Transjordan and Decapolis up the coast to Sidon and Tyre and into Syria. People in every kind of physical and spiritual distress set out to find him, and soon the crowds around him were even more cosmopolitan than the standard rich mixture of Palestine. The whole atmosphere around Jesus was charged with expectancy for extraordinary spectacle. Whenever possible Jesus would slip back into private life for a little recreation and conversation with his friends. After he had exorcised the evil spirit in Capernaum he and his companions went to Simon Peter's house to get away from the mob.

It wasn't much of a refuge because Peter's mother-in-law was in bed with a high fever. The depressing aura of illness pervaded the house. Before Peter and Andrew could do more than express surprise and concern, though, Jesus took charge. He rebuked the fever. An eminently practical way to restore the hostess and also to help Peter's mother-in-law. Good cheer returned to the house, just in time.

Word had gotten out where Jesus was, and almost as if by signal the sick of every imaginable variety from the whole countryside were brought at sunset to the house. Jesus went out into the yard in the midst of the ailing and the insane where he began to heal and to drive out demons. It was pandemonium with the evil spirits shrieking and screaming and caterwauling.

Everybody but Jesus slept late the morning after the wild, tumultuous night. When Peter got up Jesus was not there, and they had to search through the surrounding countryside until they found him praying in a lonely spot. Peter told Jesus that another crowd was gathering at the house, but Jesus was restless and ready to leave. "Let's move on to the country towns," he said. "I have to give my message there, too; this is what I came back to Galilee to do." That morning Jesus and his companions started out through Galilee, preaching in the meeting-houses and healing the sick. The pace of his ministry never let up from that time on.

[CONFLICT]

ONE OF THE fiercest arguments Jesus had with Pharisees took place early in his travels. He was preaching in Capernaum when some men came to the edge of the dense crowd around Jesus, carrying a paralyzed friend. It was impossible to get through to Jesus, so they circled the crowd and climbed to the roof of the house. Removing the tiling, they lowered the bed holding the paralytic right into the middle of the group surrounding Jesus. He was impressed with their ingenuity and said to the sick man, "Your sins are forgiven you, my friend." That did it. Jesus had thrown a challenge right into the Pharisees' teeth. Everybody there had seen people healed and doubtless they were getting accustomed to doses of the miraculous. Now Jesus astounded them by changing the terms. He did not heal the paralytic who had been dramatically presented to him—he forgave his sins.

"Who is this that speaks blasphemies? Who can forgive sins but God only?" the Pharisees argued. But they had been tricked by their own eagerness. Quick as a flash Jesus asked them, "Is it easier to say, 'Your sins are forgiven you,' or to say, 'Get up and walk?' I will prove to you then that the Son of Man has authority on earth to forgive sins." So he said to the paralytic, "I tell you, get up, pick up your bed, and go home." The man immediately got up and went home, praising God. No one knows what the paralyzed man was thinking as he lay there on his pallet with his sins forgiven before he was healed, but he probably did not take Jesus' presumption as seriously as the Pharisees did.

There were many cures in the course of the next weeks and months, but Jesus was increasingly diverted by the Pharisees and scribes or lawyers. He saw them as nit-pickers concerned more with technical observance of the laws than with spiritual matters the laws were designed to protect. They were stiff-necked guardians. Lineal descendants of Jews who had withstood the onslaught of Assyrians, Babylonians, Egyptians, Greeks and Romans, they were unbending in the face of a rambunctious individual like Jesus. As Jesus' following grew, the opposition grew and there were many who could not be persuaded there was anything good about Jesus. As the Son of Man with power to heal he was unmanageable, but as a simple blasphemer he could be destroyed. The spies and informers around him were thick as flies and they found a lot to report.

Jesus' style of life was abhorrent to Pharisees. They kept a proper distance from women, children and sinners, but Jesus gave an inordinate amount of time and affection to these three groups. Then, as now, it was harder to forgive a man who broke a social custom than a man who committed a crime. Jesus went out of his way to infuriate the establishment by cultivating a tax collector named Matthew, and actually drawing him into the inner circle of disciples. Tax collectors were frequently extortionist turncoats and chiselers—they squeezed as much money as they could from Palestinians and passed on as little as possible to the Romans.

During Jesus' lifetime taxes were very high and there was terrific resistance to paying them. Jesus passed over all of this as if just cause for the prejudice did not exist, and he ate and drank with Matthew and other collectors and their crummy friends. As a matter of fact he must have seemed as careless about who his companions were as many youth are today. He went so far as to fool around with gentiles.

It was Jesus' nature to be practical about rules governing such practices as fasting. One time both disciples of John, his baptizing cousin, and some Pharisees joined forces to question Jesus about fasting. He made it clear that his situation was such that ordinary rules could not apply to him. He also gave examples of other situations that could not be fully accommodated to old times. Certain practices would have to be relaxed. Jesus was intuitively fashioning a new religion for a new world, yet he never made any wholesale condemnation of the old.

Time did not permit his bringing everything to a screeching halt on the sabbath. If his followers were hungry on the sabbath, they picked grain from the fields and ate it. Jesus was shrewd enough to find a precedent in scripture—he reminded the Pharisees that David had gone into the temple and eaten bread offered to Yahweh —but his relaxation of rules was part and parcel of his intention to make life tolerable. "The sabbath was made for man, not man for the sabbath," he said.

On another occasion Jesus entered a meetinghouse under the watchful eyes of Pharisees and he was confronted by a man with a withered hand. Everybody in the meeting-house was looking at that poor withered hand, and the owner of it was wondering what sort of wondrous par-liamentary conflict he had gotten into. When the man became unendurably present to everyone, the lawyers asked, "Is it lawful to heal on the sabbath?" In the pres-ence of a man who might be denied health on the basis of a technicality, they forced the question. Jesus gave it back to them in the very practical terms of their avarice.

"Which of you," Jesus asked, "if he has one sheep and it falls into a pit on the sabbath will not lay hold of it and pull it out?" The economic reflex to pick a sheep out of a hole had not been snuffed out by Hebrew laws governing the sabbath. "Of how much more value is a man than a sheep." What could they say? The Phari-sees were boiling with silent anger because they had been caught in a transparently evil position. "Stretch out your hand," Jesus said to the man. And if you know about challenge, you can imagine the masculine rumble in his voice. The paralytic, caught in several circles of conflict, held out the hand. Jesus cured it. The Pharisees had had it, and they went out to plot with some Herodians how to destroy Jesus.

When the stifling air of the meetinghouses and the hectoring of the badgering Pharisees got to be more than Jesus could stand, he took to the countryside. The crowds were sticky, hard to control, and the stand-up confrontations were tiring, but the give and take was welcome after the angle shooting of the politicians. Jesus was great at the toe-to-toe hassle with the wash of humanity always available by the shore or along the road. At a time when most Jews were persnickety about whom they talked to, Jesus had an easy, casual air. He was forever striking up conversations that dismayed his followers. He would tie right into an idle scattering of drifters under the cedars, and open the conversation with that day's equivalent of "What can I do for you?"

After the sabbath disputes Jesus took his regular followers back to the Sea of Galilee. The lake had always been famous as a health resort. The shores were always loaded with invalids and convalescents. There was a built-in list of candidates for healing wherever Jesus appeared. The local deposit of demented, infectious and disabled bodies had been reinforced during this trip by ailing pilgrims from the surrounding region, city types from Jerusalem, regulars from Galilee, and a substantial contingent of folks from Judea.

Jesus depended increasingly on his staff to manage the complicated business of controlling the crowds of listeners. Each aspect of his work became more demanding. Desperate people who came long distances had to be fed or shepherded back to town before nightfall. The swelling tide of the afflicted affected his logistics, so that he had to acquire more disciples to baptize, to spread the good news, to extend his work in every way. On this occasion he saw that the crowd might crush him or push him into the water in their urge to touch him, and he got his staff to bring a boat which was anchored just off-shore. He healed people who were brought out to him and he drove out a swarm of demons that set up a terrible howling racket accusing him of being the Son of God. It was another exhausting day at the beach.

Later, Jesus walked up to a deserted hilltop and thought deeply about the men closest to him who bore part of the burden of his work. These few would be living witnesses, would share his powers, would be his cadre in a gamble that the good news could be written in the lives of his contemporaries. He chose twelve to be close to him: Simon Peter, James and John, the sons of Zebedee, whom Jesus called "men of thunder," Andrew, Philip, Bartholomew, Matthew, Thomas, James the son of Alphaeus, Thaddaeus, Simon the patriot, Judas Iscariot. He told them, "I will also send you out to preach, and you will have the power to drive out demons."

After an inspired, improvised staff meeting Jesus and his cadre came down from the hill and went back into Capernaum. From the moment they reached town they were swamped. Word had spread that a mad prophet was curing everyone in sight. Every energetic leper within five hundred miles hit the road. A horde of optimistic feeble folks started moving.

Everybody gathered at the foot of a nearby mountain where he launched into a great sermon which turned upside down everything the Jews had thought about the love of God. He praised the Law but he described a morality which went far beyond technical observance of the Law. "Do not think that I have come to do away with the Law of Moses and the teaching of the prophets," he said. "I have not come to do away with them, but to give them real meaning." It was obvious that Jesus had been guilty of creative interpretation of the Law, that he had rewritten it under the very eyes of the lawyers. But he did not want to give comfort to lawbreakers. Jesus knew that the Law provided the only orderly means of moving from the old life to a new life. He purposely ex-aggerated the point. "Remember this. As long as heaven and earth last, the least point or the smallest detail of the Law will not be done away with—not until the end of all things."

Then he took a backhand swipe. "I tell you, then, you will be able to enter the kingdom of heaven only if your standard of life is far above the standard of the teachers of the Law and the Pharisees." Get it straight, Jesus says. Obeying the Law is a necessity; worshiping it is idolatry. The words Jesus spoke must have come pouring out as cool water to the thirsty. His beatitudes would sparkle for an oppressed, melancholy audience. "Blessed are the poor in spirit. . . . Blessed are the meek. . . . Blessed are those who mourn. . . ." He blesses the human condi-tion he sees before him.

Scales must have fallen from the eyes of listeners when Jesus gave the precepts of conduct for citizens of the kingdom of God. They shine with a deep inner light. "Turn the other cheek. . . . Love your enemies. . . . Be merciful. . . . Do not save riches here on earth. . . ." Startling commandments for an avaricious century when the common man could be sold into slavery for debts, when torture for punishment and for public edification was habitual, and vengeance was eagerly satisfied. You could say that men in the first century were generally uneasy. So they were uncommonly attentive to Jesus' talk about the gate, the way, the key.

After the momentous revival meeting at the foot of the Mountain, Jesus returned to town to regroup for his mission. He now had a sense of a broadening mandate to take his ministry out into the world without necessarily excluding the gentiles out there. One of the first persons he met was a Roman centurion who was clearly enormously upset. Jesus knew that this soldier commanded about two hundred men, and that he had been appointed carefully by the Consul with the advice of the Military Tribune.

This centurion was exceptional because he had taken personal interest in the Jews and had even built them a meetinghouse in the town. He ran up to Jesus and exclaimed, "Sir, my servant is sick in bed, unable to move, and suffering terribly." "I will go and make him well," Jesus said immediately. But the officer tried to prevent Jesus from making the trip. "Lord, I am not worthy to have you come under my roof. Just give the order and my servant will get well." Jesus was amazed by this response and said to the Jewish elders who were present with the centurion, "I tell you I have never seen such faith as this in anyone in Israel."

The man's faith was a revelation to Jesus. Jesus was coming to understand that the Good News was good news for everybody. The zealously guarded Jewish religion would be turned loose to the despised gentiles. The faith would be kept not by hoarding it but by giving it away. It would not be easy to convince the disciples of this. The great ingathering instinct had to be reversed.

"Remember this!" Jesus said to his staff. "Many will come from the east and the west and sit down at the table in the kingdom of heaven with Abraham, Isaac and Jacob. But those who should be in the Kingdom will be thrown out into the darkness outside, where they will cry and gnash their teeth."

Turning to the centurion he said, "Go home, and what you believe will be done for you." When the man returned to his home, he found his servant healed.

Sometime later, Jesus walked to a city called Nain located a few miles southwest of Mount Tabor in southern Galilee. As he and his followers approached the main gate to the stone-walled city they met a huge funeral procession. Word quickly passed to Jesus' party that the only son of a widowed woman had died. A common, if pathetic, situation, but Jesus was compassionate. "Don't cry," he told the wailing woman. He touched the coffin and the men carrying it stopped. With great authority Jesus said, "Young man! Get up, I tell you." The dead man, Luke reports, sat up and began talking. This was a very different matter from curing a disease or routing a demon. Everyone was filled with both praise of God and fear of Jesus, and word went out that God had come to save his people.

This kind of dramatic episode certainly made Jesus' views about eternal life a lot more convincing. His cousin John's disciples heard the news right away and they passed it on to John in prison. John had been thinking about Jesus ever since the baptism but he had of course not confronted Jesus directly since then. The story of a dead man brought back to life couldn't be ignored.

John's followers found Jesus and identified themselves and asked John's question, "Are you the one he said was going to come, or should we expect someone else?" Jesus had great respect for John's role in the scheme of things. He gave his answer in the form of a marathon healing session. He healed many sick persons and drove out evil spirits. Then he said to John's emissaries, "Go back and tell John what you have seen and heard: the blind can see, the lame can walk, the lepers are made clean, the deaf can hear, the dead are raised to life, and the good news is preached to the poor."

"Remember this!" Jesus told the emotionally over-wrought crowd in the open marketplace of Nain. "John the Baptist is greater than any man who has ever lived." There was confusion apparent in their faces, the same confusion which the scribes and Pharisees reflected when they asked John, "Are you the Messiah? Are you Elijah?" Then Jesus added, "But he who is least in the kingdom of God is greater than he." Jesus had put John's mind at rest about the great question which tormented him.

While he was in the mood Jesus took on his whole generation and lambasted them with sarcastic scorn. They were like a group of children shouting taunts at each other in the schoolyard. They were fickle and feckless. They said John was a madman because he wouldn't drink wine, and then they said Jesus was a drunkard and glutton because he ate and drank with sinners. They were useless. Then Jesus excoriated the cities, particularly those cities where the people had not changed their ways even after he had performed miracles. He consigned

Capernaum to hell. Then, feeling much more cheerful, Jesus went to dinner.

The invitation to dinner had come from a Pharisee named Simon who was fascinated by the stories about Jesus. Jesus, exhausted with the terrible chore of trying to bring people to the truth, was hungry for a little social life. He arrived and settled down with considerable relief for a relaxed evening. But he was not spared for long. A woman from the town tracked him down and she was through the door and behind Jesus before his host was aware of what was happening. Now Jesus was on a couch at right angles to the table in the fashion of the time, with his feet away from the table. The woman leaned over his feet with her hair pouring down and she wept a flood of tears on his feet.

The attention was ironic on the face of it because Simon had neglected the ordinary courtesy of having water brought around for Jesus to wash his hands and feet. And now here was this woman, whom Simon knew to be a notorious sinner, wiping Jesus' feet with her hair and tears. She kissed Jesus' feet and anointed them with an aromatic ointment from an alabaster flask concealed in her garments. Irritated and put off by this scene, Simon thought to himself that if Jesus really were a prophet he would recognize the character of this woman and be repelled by her. Jesus read his expression.

"Simon, I have something to say to you." "What is it, Teacher?" Simon asked, reassuming his responsibilities as host. Jesus told him about the creditor who had two debtors; one owed him five hundred dollars, the other fifty dollars. Neither could pay, and he canceled the obligations of both. "Which one will love him more?" Jesus asked. Simon reluctantly guessed it would be the man with the larger debt. "Correct," Jesus said. Then, as Simon knew he would, he pointed to the woman.

"Do you see this woman? I came into your house, and you gave me no water for my feet, but she has washed my feet with her tears and dried them with her hair. You did not welcome me with a kiss, but she has not stopped kissing my feet since I came. You provided no oil for my head, but she has covered my feet with perfume. I tell you, then, the great love she has shown proves that her many sins are forgiven. Whoever has been forgiven little, however, shows only a little love." Jesus turned to the woman. "Your sins are forgiven," he said. There was muttering around the table about his "forgiving sins." Without any elaborate admonition Jesus said to her, "Your faith has saved you. Go in peace."

After this brief respite Jesus and his twelve assistants struck out through the nearby towns and villages preaching the good news about the kingdom of God. On this trip a number of women who had been healed of evil spirits and diseases accompanied the group. Among them were Mary Magdalene who had been freed from seven demons; Joanna, the wife of Chuza who was an officer in Herod's court; a woman named Susanna, and others. It took some sort of commitment in that strict culture for a woman to cut herself loose from society and follow such a perilous course. Yet this new contingent of helpers surely made a striking difference. The instinct for nurturing and attending to domestic details was gratefully received by this beleaguered band.

The onslaught of the crowds, the building commotion of the campaign, the frenzied demands for healing all turned Jesus' life into an endurance contest. He had to slip into the wilderness to have any chance to think. He was swept into a bottomless sea of human misery and hope, and he existed in a delirium of ministration.

When his family heard all the reports they set out to get him because people were saying that Jesus was mad. Before they arrived Jesus healed a man possessed by a demon who could not see or speak. It was a sure crowd pleaser because madness horrified them more than any other ailment. Those who witnessed the healing asked in awe, "Can this be the Son of David?" But the Pharisees, who were provoked and outraged by these healing scenes, counterattacked: "He drives out demons only because their ruler Beelzebub gave him power to do so." That started a fierce debate.

Jesus argued that if Satan had given him power to drive out demons, then Satan's kingdom was split and would soon fall. He said it was in the nature of things for a divided country or household to collapse. "How can Satan cast out Satan?" he asked. Then he said to them, "It is God's spirit who gives me the power to drive out demons, which proves that the kingdom of God has already come upon you."

Jesus understood the implications of the charge that his power came from Beelzebub. And he had just about had enough of that sort of commentary. He turned on the Pharisees and leveled a terrible threat that changed all the rules of the game. If they wanted to say that God's power was Satan's power, they were saying an evil thing against God. "For this reason I tell you," Jesus said, "men can be forgiven any sin and any evil thing they say; but whoever says evil things against the Holy Spirit will not be forgiven. Anyone who says something against the Son of Man will be forgiven; but whoever says something against the Holy Spirit will not be forgiven—now or ever."

This sounds like overkill. Jesus has taken an implacable stand that does not allow for change of heart or mind. It may have been more threat than judgment, but there is a finality in the attack. "You snakes," he charges, "how can you say good things when you are evil? For the mouth speaks what the heart is full of. A good man brings good things out of his treasure of good things; a bad man brings bad things out of his treasure of bad things." This is the relentless Jesus who gives no quarter to the adversary. He declares all-out war to the finish. When Jesus says there will be no forgiveness for his attackers among the Pharisees he knows there will be no forgiveness for him as far as they are concerned.

Just as the debate has reached a peak, Jesus gets word that his mother and brothers are outside asking for him. The eternal impossible timing of the arrival of one's family can be the lot of any man, but Jesus got it at the worst possible time. "Your mother and brothers are standing outside, and they want to see you," the messenger said insistently. Jesus stood him down, and took this opportunity to separate himself from his earthly family "My mother and brothers are those who hear the word of God and obey it," he said.

That same day Jesus left the town and began to teach

by the sea. Here he honed the parables that stuck in the minds of the simple people he preached to, and that he became so famous for. Jesus talked to them in the language of the familiar parts of the land and the sea. The concepts were new to his listeners but the story patterns were old and comfortable. He made it clear that he wanted the dullest and sleepiest man to understand his message. The battle had been joined with the educated scribes and Pharisees who had arbitrarily rejected the teaching. The good news therefore had to be planted in common soil where it would bear fruit a hundredfold. Behind all his stories is a wisdom that leads people great distances in new directions along paths that have the appearance of complete familiarity. His repetition of these basic stories often bored his staff and made them irritable. Sometimes they paid so little attention that Jesus discovered they had missed the point, and he would patiently explain the meaning of a story in other terms.

Exhausted from a long teaching session, Jesus gave a signal in the boat where he had been standing to preach, and his disciples raised the sail. Jesus curled up in the stern and immediately fell asleep. One of those sudden treacherous storms arose with the wind blowing down the lake from the north, roiling the water and battering everything afloat. Jesus slept peacefully until the terrified disciples awakened him. "Master, we are about to die! Do you not care if we perish?" Jesus woke easily and rebuked the sea: "Peace! Be still!" The wind died into a calm. Then Jesus said to them, "Why are you so frightened? Why is it that you don't have faith?" And Mark reports that they were terribly afraid and said to one another, "Who is this man? Even the wind and waves obey him!" As the calm settled the sea Jesus thought about the incredible difficulties of getting the staff to understand or remember things. It was as if they had been born each day with no memory, and although they shared deeply in his life, at times they seemed entirely innocent of what it was all about.

There was no serenity ahead where they landed in the territory of the Gerasenes. When Jesus stepped out of the boat he was accosted by a notorious raving maniac, a celebrated local character. This naked man had been living in the burial caves at the top of the hill for a long time. Nobody had the temerity to approach him or the strength to subdue him. There were pieces of chain still on his arms and legs from the futile attempts made to bind him. Day and night he wandered among the graves and through the hills caterwauling and cutting himself with stones. It was as if Jesus and this madman had met by prearranged signal. The real miracle was that Jesus would calmly face this crazed man when every instinct said run for it. But it was typical of him that he took this hairy bit of business as his personal project.

"What is your name?" Jesus asked. "Legion," the madman answered, for many demons had been in him. Very calmly, without any fear or boggling, Jesus began to talk with him. It was probably the first time in years that anyone had tried to cope with this man or had treated him as a human being. The disciples, meanwhile, had taken the boat out into the lake where they waited nervously for Jesus. There was a struggle between Jesus and the uproar inside the madman. Everything was deathly still and quiet, and then there was a swirling rush of air. A herd of swine feeding nearby suddenly bolted and ran wild, as if possessed. In a great avalanche they plunged over a cliff into the lake. The whole herd drowned as everybody watched. The swineherds were stupefied at this disaster, and they scattered across the countryside recounting the episode to anyone who would listen. Many people came swarming to the scene excitedly discussing several hundred different versions of what had happened. There they found the madman sitting with Jesus, clothed and in his right mind. Sure enough, the carcasses of drowned pigs were bobbing around in the water. The man begged Jesus to let him go with him, but Jesus said, "Return to your home and declare how much God has done for you." And the man did go through the Ten Towns of the Decapolis telling his story.

That was strong medicine for the neighborhood, and after all the facts were indisputably settled a deputation of local citizens asked Jesus to please leave their territory. The Gerasenes did not want all of Jesus' business. So he and his followers pushed off and sailed to the other side of the lake. This time it was a pleasant trip. They were met by a large gathering, among whom was a man of obvious prominence. It was Jairus, an official at the local meetinghouse. "My little daughter is very sick, she is dying. Please come," he implored Jesus, "and place your hands on her, so that she will get well." "Let's go," Jesus said.

The group including Jesus and Jairus pressed through a mob waiting to see Jesus. One determined woman forced her way after them, sensed the route, and with agility made her way close to Jesus. "If I just touch his clothes, if I just touch his clothes . . ." she gasped, and she did manage to touch the edge of his robe. "Who touched my clothes?" Jesus asked the crowd. It seemed a ridiculous question to the staff because everybody was crowding around. But Jesus kept staring into the crowd to see who had done it. The woman who touched him had been bleeding terribly for twelve years. None of the local healers had done her any good; she had spent all her money on them, and she only got worse. When she realized that the bleeding had suddenly stopped, she came forward trembling with fright. Jesus said to her, "My daughter, your faith has made you well. Go in peace, and be healed from your trouble." None of the aloofness that men generally have in the face of women's problems characterized Jesus' attitude. He overcame the contemporary rabbis' inclinations to stay away from women.

But this was only an interlude to the main event of the day. Jairus still had to be attended to. While they walked, messengers from Jairus' house arrived breathlessly and told their master, "Your daughter has died. Why should you bother the Teacher any longer?" Jesus paid no attention to them. Typically, he understood the difference between his problem and their problem, and he didn't waste any words. Jesus singled out Peter, James and John to accompany him as they reached the house. "Why all this confusion? Why are you crying? The child is not dead—she is only sleeping," he said to the crazed mourners. But they ridiculed him. Jesus drove everyone out of the house except the parents and his three disciples. He went to the girl and said, "Little girl! Get up, I tell you." She got up at once and began walking around.

Girls were not ordinarily very highly esteemed in Palestine at that time, but Jairus was particularly devoted
to his twelve-year-old daughter. She meant everything to
her father, and since Jesus didn't share the hangups about
girls being inferior, he had an uncomplicated view of the
situation. The people reacted to these developments with
both dismay and joy. Jesus said, "Give her something to
eat." And this time he gave strict order to his staff
not to tell other people about this episode. It is so typical
of Jesus that he reminded the father to give the child
something to eat. He knew that death was a very de-
pleting experience, and that a person brought back from
death would have a voracious appetite. The whole episode
had a personal stamp, as if Jesus had indulged himself
because he could not bear to think of this twelve-year-old
girl being dead.

At this stage in his teaching, Jesus began to bring his
staff closer and closer to everything he did and said
and thought. He had the same problems everybody has
with associates or partners, but the nature of his gamble
made it crucial that cadre be able to take over. He re-
hearsed them and reprimanded them and sometimes despaired of them, but he never did accept the very real
evidence that they might not be able to manage. He
looked at them with a hopeful heart, not with a critical
mind, for frail though they were, his disciples were all
that he had to help carry the good news.

Slowly and imperfectly, the twelve had begun to in-
ternalize the qualities and characteristics of Jesus. They
had had all along an instinctual feeling for his holiness

and authority, and gradually they began to understand from him the progressive revelation that if man would repent of his sins and accept God, he would be born anew and have eternal life. This glorious, improbable message was too much to accept once and for all—they had to relive again and again what was incandescently displayed before their eyes day after day. It would not be clear until the very end whether the lesson would take or not.

But the time had come for a field test. Jesus called his staff together and commissioned them to go out and work on the road. He gave them power over evil spirits and the power to heal the sick. As part of their walking orders, Jesus said, "Do not go into any Gentile territory or any Samaritan towns. Go instead to the lost sheep of the people of Israel. Go and preach, 'The kingdom of heaven is near.' Heal the sick, raise the dead, make the lepers clean, drive out demons. You have received without paying, so give without being paid. Do not carry any gold, silver or copper money in your pockets; do not carry a beggar's bag for the trip or an extra shirt, or shoes, or a walking stick. A worker should be given what he needs."

Jesus started them out with their homefolks but he told them to live off the land. He told the disciples with great confidence that they should look for welcome in each town or village and stay with the person who welcomed them until they left that place. But if they were not welcomed, Jesus said, they should leave, shaking the dust of that place off their feet.

There was no flimflam about Jesus. He gave his disciples the most downbeat inspirational send-off in religious history. It was a momentous assignment, but Jesus made no bones about the treatment they were going to receive. "I am sending you just like sheep to a pack of wolves. You must be as cautious as snakes and as gentle as doves. Watch out, for there will be men who will arrest you and take you to court, and they will whip you in their meeting houses."

He sent them out like commando teams, two by two, urging them not to depend on their own words but to let the spirit of the Father speak through them. Jesus had to infuse in them a will to survive. It was not enough that they should fight to the death for their beliefs. They must live to the death for their beliefs, and then death itself should be a witness. Jesus turns finally to the gut question of loyalty: "Whoever confesses publicly that he belongs to me, I will do the same for him before my Father in Heaven. But whoever denies publicly that he belongs to me, then I will deny him before my Father in Heaven." In the conclusion of his briefing, Jesus talked as if his disciples were all in a suicide mission—it is an unremitting charge. Only a tough commander who knew that he faced a much more certain fate himself could so decisively lay down the ground rules for his staff.

His briefing shows Jesus to be an unflinching realist. It is going to be hard sell all the way. So he reassures his newly commissioned missionaries that he understands that their words and acts will not be accepted uniformly, that they will be setting sons against their fathers, daughters against their mothers, families against families. This discipleship is a consecrated life that allows no other major commitments, and Jesus severs his staff from past ties to their families. "Whoever loves his father or mother more than me is not worthy of me," he says. "Whoever does not take up his cross and follow in my steps is not worthy of me. Whoever tries to gain his own life will lose it; whoever loses his life for my sake will gain it."

Jesus realizes now that they are traveling on one-way tickets, that the implications in the ministry of spreading the good news are persecution and death. Salvation is the ultimate consideration and if you say that you have a corner on it then everybody else is selling second-rate goods. Either Jesus was a blasphemer or the holy men were out of business. Unless his cures came from Beelze-bub, he had cut off the Pharisees with no escape hatch. This was a radical, reckless faith that Jesus was pushing, and if it caught on the Jewish institutions were going to be bypassed on the new route to the kingdom. But the Jewish rulers who had stood against every other threat in the past were not going to give way before Jesus. That became very clear.

Word came at this point, that John the Baptizer had been beheaded by Herod's guard. Not much of a diplo-mat, John had condemned Herod initially for fooling around with his brother Philip's wife, Herodias, and more sternly later for marrying Herodias. Herod clapped John into prison but he kept him safe because he knew John was a righteous and holy man. As a matter of fact, Herod went in for mind-bending experiences and he was always glad to talk with John. This oracular and prophetic man impressed and frightened him. Herod didn't like what John said, but he couldn't keep away from him. This meant that John got comparatively good treatment in prison and was allowed to have friends and disciples visit him from the outside.

The peculiar relationship of the corrupt king and ascetic prophet was too highly charged to last. A typical indulgence of Herod's brought it to an end. During one of the great pagan banquets that Herod held—this one happened to be in celebration of his own birthday—the king was showing off before his courtiers and the officials of Galilee. He requested that Herodias' daughter dance for the assembly. She wasn't Herodias' daughter for nothing, and it must have been one wild fandango because everybody loved it. In a grandiose gesture Herod told the breathless girl that she could have anything. "Even if you ask for half of my kingdom, I will give it to you."

"Ask for the head of John the baptizer," her mother demanded. Salome was intrigued with the novelty of this and made her request.

"I want you to give me at once the head of John the baptizer on a platter," she said. Herod was shocked by the request but he was a proud man and could not go back on his word in the presence of his court. So he sent for John's head and it was delivered on a platter. The girl gave the head to her mother who seemed already to have lost interest in it.

When Jesus heard the news, he gathered his staff and set out in a boat to a place named Bethsaida where they could grieve for John and meditate on what had happened. They left without announcement because the crowds had given them no privacy to talk or reflect. But word spread that they were going in the direction of Bethsaida and by the time their boat got there another crowd had gathered and people were pouring in.

Jesus resigned himself to the situation and talked to the people about the kingdom of God and healed many of the ill. There was no end to it, and as always, the end of the day came before the end of the procession of the afflicted. The staff urged Jesus to send the people into the nearby villages for lodging and food for they had gathered in a lonely place, but Jesus felt they should be fed there. The followers checked the stores and told Jesus there were only five loaves of bread and two fishes.

"What are we going to do?" they asked. "Go into the village and buy supplies for this mob?" Jesus suggested that they be seated in companies of about fifty each. He took the loaves and the fishes and looked up to heaven and blessed and broke them and gave them to the disciples to serve to the crowd. All ate and were satisfied, and when it came time to clean up, there were twelve baskets of broken pieces left over. The amazed staff made an honest effort to judge the size of the group and they agreed that there had been five thousand men eating with them that night.

Jesus was having a more and more impactive effect on the crowds that he preached to. He was transporting them and moving them so deeply that they followed him heedlessly the way sheep follow their shepherd. They were beginning to worship him like a king. He was aware of this adoration and it disturbed him. The day had given Jesus a great deal to think about. That John should die because of a pixilated dancing girl and the frivolous

whim of a drunken, second-rate king was not comfort-
ing. John was a prophet and prophets carried their heads
with uncertainty. But it seemed to be clear that God
was not going to interpose himself to establish a kingdom
on earth. As for the hysteria of the crowd that Jesus
had fed—how could they be saved from their own
passionate delusion that Jesus could save them through
political leadership in a mightly revolt against oppression?
Certain things were not to happen on earth.

After the people had been satisfied with preaching, food
and miracles, they were sent away and Jesus went off
into the hills by himself to pray. Many things were
coming together in his head. The feverish response of
the crowd was suddenly translated for him into insight
that popular success was not the point of his work. The
insight unsettled him when he thought about the lack of
understanding on the part of his disciples who were
always thinking in very tangible terms. What did the
death of John and other signs mean?

As Jesus prayed and the night wore on, he had a sudden feeling of alarm about his followers whom he had
sent ahead of him in the boat to Bethsaida. When Jesus
looked out over the waters of the Sea of Galilee, it was
between three and six o'clock in the morning and he
could see that the disciples had not made much progress.
They had taken down the sails because of a high wind
and were frantically rowing the boat through the breaking waves. So Jesus started out across the water and overtook them in the storm. Their nerves already screwed
tight by the struggle with the storm, they were staggered
at first sight of him.

"It's a ghost," they screamed. They could believe there was a ghost there, but they could not recognize Jesus. Then he spoke to them: "Take courage! It's me, don't be afraid." Then he got into the boat and the wind died down. They were utterly confused. Jesus realized then that they had not understood the feeding of the people with loaves and fishes; their minds could not grasp it. Neither could they believe that he could come after them walking on the water. It was not entirely certain that they would ever understand anything. But Jesus' deep good humor kept the question stable in his mind and, as he examined it, he saw the odds of his gamble in a hard, bright light. Man with his awesome instability had every imperfection and every capacity for failure and inconstancy, but there was no limit to his soaring. As he could fail, he could rise with high lift and low drag to the very gates of heaven. The possibility of the divine lies within the miraculous expansion of the ordinary. Man could be like God, and he had to be like God to be the Son of God. It was a calculated risk, but Jesus had decided to gamble everything on the possibility of measureless change inside the consciousness of ordinary man.

Tens of thousands had heard Jesus preach and had seen his miracles, and yet he knew these people would always be hungry for new signs. Most would forget and fall from faith. They could neither believe what they saw nor remember what they had believed. It seemed to him best to put the lesson harshly and relentlessly to them and let the dropouts go.

Once, in Capernaum, he took the crowd on a rocketing trip of the imagination in order to spin off the ones who would not go the distance. Among other things he told them: "I tell you the truth: he who believes has eternal life. I am the bread of life. Your ancestors ate the manna in the desert, but died. But the bread which comes down from heaven is such that whoever eats it will not die. I am the living bread which came down from heaven. If anyone eats this bread he will live forever. And the bread which I will give him is my flesh, which I give so that the world may live."

People left in droves. Many of his disciples grumbled and said this teaching was too hard. Jesus replied calmly, in effect, "Take it or leave it." He asked his most intimate followers whether they would like to leave also. Simon Peter answered for the group: "Lord, to whom would we go? You have the words that give eternal life. And now we believe and know that you are the Holy One from God." Jesus replied grimly that although he had personally chosen all twelve of his immediate staff, " . . . one of you is a devil." The disciples could hardly cope with this comment. They had seen the faithful drift away and had felt anxiety over their own choices. Perhaps each believer in the group felt some safety in the fact that there was one traitor among them. "At least I don't have the weakest loyalty in the group," each one could say to himself.

The scribes and the Pharisees may have been tormented by the temperament of Jesus and nettled by everything he said, but they couldn't stay away from him. Being themselves obsessed with rules, they querulously challenged Jesus on his and his disciples' technical violations of the tradition of the elders. While the great fundamental concepts of Judaism were in contest, the Pharisees staged a full-scale debate about which foods were clean and how one should wash one's hands in order to eat them. During a hostile exchange between Jesus and his antagonists, Jesus lost his temper and dismissed the whole subject with a wild, heretical statement which he then repeated and elaborated to the crowd.

"Listen and understand!" he told them. "It is not what goes into a person's mouth that makes him unclean; rather, what comes out of it makes him unclean." The disciples told Jesus he had hurt the Pharisees' feelings, and then they admitted that they didn't understand either. "You are no more intelligent than the others," Jesus said despairingly, and then he carefully explained. "Don't you understand? Anything that goes into a person's mouth goes into his stomach and then on out of the body. But the things that come out of the mouth have come from the heart; such things make a man unclean. For from his heart come the evil ideas which lead him to kill, commit adultery and do other immoral things, rob and tell lies and slanders about others. These are the things that make a man unclean."

In taking this extreme position, Jesus was profaning the sacred rules of Jewish religious behavior in order to build his theme of the supreme importance of the inner man. It was the integrity, the conviction, the reality in the heart of man, not the ritual or the observances, that was important. Man could be damned for lust in his mind or murder in his heart, but not for failing to wash his hands properly before eating a guinea hen. Jesus is methodically clearing away the underbrush between man and God.

When Peter remarks that the feelings of Jewish authorities are hurt, Jesus says, "Don't worry about them! They
are blind leaders and when one blind man leads another,
both fall in the ditch." "You have a clever way of reject-
ing God's law in order to uphold your own teaching,"
he once said to the Pharisees.

The growing desire to make Jesus a king—by force if
necessary—and the growing unmanageability of the
crowds made it impossible for him to work around Bethsaida and Capernaum. The lawyers were getting stickier
every day, and the whole atmosphere was ominous, so
Jesus decided he would let the situation cool in Galilee
while he broadened his work. He must also have realized
how much his followers had to learn about the gentiles
and their real prejudices toward the gentiles. So he took
them north into Phoenicia, to the areas around Tyre and
Sidon on the Mediterranean coast. It is likely that Jesus
and his group took the Great Trunk Road south and
then turned westward on the minor road that led to
Accho, and from there they would have taken the Water-
Parting route along the coast to Tyre and thence north
to Sidon.

Near Tyre Jesus tried to take refuge in a friendly
home. But there was to be no rest in privacy. A Canaan-
ite woman who had been born in Phoenicia found him
out and when she was not admitted to his presence she
shrieked for him and would not shut up despite the
threats of the staff. The commotion finally reached Jesus'
attention and he came to the door. "Son of David, Sir!"
she cried. "Have mercy on me! My daughter has a demon
and is in a terrible condition." Jesus did not say a word

but he watched the disciples to see what they would do. "Send her away," they said angrily. "She is following us and making all this noise!" Then Jesus silenced her. He said harshly, "I have been sent only to the lost sheep of the people of Israel." But the woman came and fell at his feet. "Help me, Sir!" she implored. Caricaturing the insular attitudes of the disciples, Jesus said, "It isn't right to take the children's food and throw it to the dogs." "That is right, Sir," she answered quickly. "But even the dogs eat the leftovers that fall from their master's table." Jesus' eyes shone. "You are a woman of great faith! What you want will be done for you," he said warmly. And at that very moment her daughter was healed.

The miracles are striking, but they are not essential. You can forget the miracles, but you can't forget the message. The good news about the Kingdom was the major miracle. This is the miracle that would keep performing itself over and over again.

With Jesus came a new age. John the baptizer introduced it when he said, "The Kingdom is at hand." Jesus followed this with a more urgent message: "The Kingdom is now!" The great mandate is to love God, and to love one's fellow man.

Jesus said, "The Law of Moses and the writings of the prophets were in effect up to the time of John the baptizer; since then the good news about the Kingdom of God is being told, and everyone forces his way in." And, again, he said, "The Kingdom of God does not come in such a way as to be seen. No one will say, 'Look, here it is!' or 'There it is!'; because the Kingdom of God is within you."

The immense question is, "How do you get into the Kingdom? How do you make it with God?" Jesus answers, "You do nothing!" This is the good news. "Have faith, only believe!" Jesus enjoined the people he healed. It was his way of saying, "Don't sweat it." He says, "Ask and you will receive; seek and you will find; knock and the door will be opened to you." This is a radically different view of God. This God even goes out after you. This is the point of the parable of the prodigal son.

The parables show Jesus' evolving understanding of the Kingdom. He says, "It is like a mustard seed which a man took and planted in his field; the plant grew and became a tree, and the birds made their nests in its branches." It is the efficacy of the active principle that works within. Mighty and mysterious potentials are hidden in tiny and almost invisible beginnings.

Jesus used parables to invent new truth out of old understanding. He earnestly told them to his disciples, and despaired. They never seemed to understand his point. They were followers, not protectors. They dawdled in emergencies; bolted and fled in peril; and, he knew some would finally deny him or worse. Jesus railed against them; prayed over them; and took the awful gamble that somehow they would pull themselves together, and, with the help of God, prevail. These disciples would have to take the message, the good news, and with it change the world.

[REVELATION]

JESUS HAD COME to a crisis in his work, and he knew it. He had precipitated a boiling political crisis in Palestine that was building every day. To cool it a little and gain time, he took his companions up through northern Galilee to the town of Caesarea Philippi, a lovely ancient town renowned in the first century for its lush greenness even at the height of the searing summer, and blessed with ample cold water flowing out of the rocks. The frontiers of Israel, Syria and Phoenicia came together there in Jesus' time just as Syria, Lebanon and Israel meet there today. It had originally been called Laish, and the people of Dan had smote and burned it. Abraham had come this way pursuing the tribesmen who had captured his nephew. Pagan groups thereabouts had called the city the abode of the gods on account of its beauty and, perhaps, of its temples to both Caesar and Pan.

When Jesus settled down on the grassy slopes near the town he undertook an interrogation of his followers. He asked what people were saying about who he was. The staff said that some people compared him to his cousin John, others to Elijah, others to Jeremiah. "What about you?" he asked them. "Who do you say I am?" Simon Peter spoke. "You are the Messiah, the Son of the living God."

"Simon, son of John, you are happy indeed!" Jesus said. "For this truth did not come to you from any human being, but it was given to you directly from my Father in heaven. And so I tell you: you are a rock, Peter, and on this rock I will build my church. Not even death will ever be able to overcome it. I will give you the keys of the kingdom of heaven: what you prohibit on earth will be prohibited in heaven; what you permit on earth will be permitted in heaven." Then Jesus ordered his group not to talk with others about this messianic conversation.

This was one of the few times Jesus was overwhelmed by the insight of the disciple. He was himself still fight-ing his way through the ambiguities, the perplexities, the cloudy, dark riddles of his identity and destiny. Like any man growing up, he had searched for himself through the forests and the deserts of his mind. But unlike other men he had to go beyond finding himself as a man. His visions and epiphanies were soul-shaking experiences that any mortal would avoid if he had the choice. There had been a sharp turn of events and now Jesus knew he would have to take his path into the whole dark side of the future. Painstakingly he began to build a vision of a new reality in their minds. Time seemed almost to dissolve before it could be spent. There was a foreshortening of time to think and teach, and of life itself.

He spoke as plainly as he could. "I must go to Jerusa-lem and suffer much from the elders, the chief priests, and the teachers of the Law. I will be put to death, and on the third day I will be raised to life." This was un-acceptable on the face of it, and everything the disciples had grudgingly learned and secretly dreamed of was un-done by it. Peter took him aside and began to rebuke him: "This must never happen to you."

Jesus turned on him in a flash. "Get away from me Satan!" he said to Peter. "You are an obstacle in my way, for these thoughts of yours are men's thoughts, not God's." In part, Jesus must have been talking to himself when he lashed out at Peter. He couldn't himself accept the total reality of this vision and he would not be free of struggling with it for a long time. If this voice that had been in Peter had been in Jesus, too, then it was the cry of every man who shouts down an impossible truth. Then Jesus laid it on the line with them. "If anyone wants to come with me, he must forget himself, carry his cross, and follow me. For the man who wants to save his own life will lose it; but the man who loses his life for my sake will find it."

From this point on the great emphasis was to prepare for the fateful days. Jesus could not refrain from healing and he could not stop preaching the good news, but in the spinaway of diminishing time he was preoccupied with completing the cycle of his influence on the disciples. About six days after Jesus had revealed the future to his staff, he took Peter and James and John with him, and together they climbed a high mountain for a brief but intensive retreat. They were entirely alone in this high isolation where they fasted and prayed. Certainly they had extensive discussion about God's will and Jesus' own messianic role. While they were there they saw a change come over Jesus. His face shone like the sun and his gar' ments became as white as light. They saw Moses and Elijah appear and talk with Jesus. Both were wrapped in heavenly glory and discussed with Jesus how he would soon fulfill God's purpose by dying in Jerusalem.

Peter and the other two were drowsy in the charged air and they could barely keep from dozing off, but Peter managed to say to Jesus, "Master, it is a good thing that we are here. Let us make three tents, one for you, one for Moses, and one for Elijah." After he spoke, half in a dream, a bright cloud overshadowed them. A voice called from the cloud, "This is my beloved son; listen to him." Suddenly they were alone with Jesus again.

When they had climbed down to the foot of the moun' tain, Jesus saw the rest of his staff talking with a large crowd. Some teachers of the Law were arguing with two of the disciples. Everyone was surprised to see Jesus, and his group ran up to him bringing a stranger. Jesus wanted to know what they were all arguing about. The stranger spoke up quickly: "Teacher, I brought my son to you because he has an evil spirit in him and cannot talk." Obviously, the man was relieved to see Jesus, the boss healer, because it was clear that he had not gotten satis' faction from the disciples. He repeated to Jesus a case history of his son who when attacked by the spirit would fall to the ground, foam at the mouth, grit his teeth, and become stiff all over. "I asked your disciples to drive the spirit out, but they could not." He sounded almost like a man complaining to one doctor about another. But Jesus was thinking about the failure of his disciples. "How un' believing you people are," he said to them in front of the crowd. "How long must I stay with you? How long do I have to put up with you? Bring the boy to me." Jesus spoke with irritation of a man who had seen his subordinates do a bad job of work. At that point the child was seized with one of his fits.

"How long has he been like this?" Jesus asked the father. The father said the fits had been occurring ever since his son was an infant and that the boy had almost died on occasion by falling into the fire or into the water. "Have pity on us and help us, if you possibly can." "Yes, said Jesus, "if *you* can!" Jesus bounced it right back to him and you have to think that if it hadn't been an object lesson for the disciples, he would have dispatched the father with his epileptic son. "Everything is possible for the person who has faith," Jesus told the father. The father at once cried out, "I do have faith, but not enough. Help me!" The crowd was closing in on them, so Jesus gave a command to the evil spirit to come out from the boy. With a scream the spirit threw the boy into a bad fit and departed. The boy was so still as he lay there that everybody said, "He's dead." But Jesus took the boy by the hand and helped him rise.

It had been a real ordeal, and Jesus was relieved and exhausted when it was over. The man didn't have enough faith, and according to Jesus' criterion, if you didn't have faith you didn't get healed. But the disciples had blundered ahead and blown the job, and the leader had to rescue the credibility of the group. It was just bad luck that they had gotten this tough case the minute Jesus' back was turned.

After they had gone indoors, the disciples asked him privately, "Why couldn't we drive the spirit out?" Jesus answered very gently, "Only prayer can drive this kind out; nothing else can." This group failure is reminiscent of Peter's attempt to walk on the water. When the chips were down the disciples had lost their nerve. In the days following, Jesus and his disciples went back down through Galilee to the northern shores of the Sea of Galilee, and they did not reveal their destination, but kept to themselves so that they could have some private conversation. Jesus took advantage of this opportunity to tell them again what lay in store for him. They listened as incredulously as ever.

Jesus felt full of playfulness when the trip was over. Peter presented him with the first opportunity to show it. The collectors of the Temple tax had come to Peter and had asked pointedly, "Does your Teacher pay the Temple tax?" Peter was smart enough to keep Jesus from getting caught in some simple-minded tax trap. "Yes, he does." When he mentioned it to Jesus, Jesus said half-jokingly, "What do you think, Simon? From whom do kings of the earth take toll or tribute? From their sons or from others?" When Peter said, "From others," Jesus told him, "Then the sons are free. However, not to give offense to them, go to the sea and cast a hook, and take the first fish that comes up. You will find in his mouth a coin that will pay for your Temple tax and for mine." Being a fisherman, Peter got a great kick out of this and he told the story as long as he lived.

The disciples were in a feisty mood because of the strains and uncertainties of the week, and they got to arguing among themselves as to which of them was the greatest. Jesus was amazed when he caught the drift of the conversation. He called a child standing nearby to come over to them, and said, "Remember this! Unless you change and become like children you will never enter the kingdom of heaven. The greatest in the kingdom of heaven is the one who humbles himself and becomes like this child. And the person who welcomes in my name one such child as this, welcomes me."

Jewish families of Jesus' time liked children, took good care of them, and educated them, but it was unusual to see a teacher or rabbi pay much attention to children. Just as he was always gentle to women and solicitous of them, Jesus paid very close attention to children. He treated them with respect and gave dire warnings to those who might harm them. It was more than his concern for the helpless that he expressed in his great sermon at the foot of the mountain. Jesus saw the incredible potential in children and he gave them the sort of dignity that we do today—childhood was a time when the inner person could be dreadfully harmed, and woe to him who did harm to the inner self of a child.

Still holding the child in his arms, Jesus told again the parable of the one sheep out of a hundred that had gone astray. "What will a man do who has a hundred sheep and one of them gets lost? He will leave the other ninety-nine grazing on the hillside and will go look for the lost sheep. When he finds it, he feels far happier over the recovery of one sheep than over the safety of the ninety-nine that did not get lost. In just the same way your

Father in heaven does not want any of these little ones to be lost."

Not long after this conversation, some people brought children for him to touch, and the disciples scolded them. Jesus was indignant at this and said, "Let the children come to me; do not try to stop them; for the kingdom of God belongs to such as these. Whoever does not accept the kingdom of God like a child will never enter it." And he put his arms around them and blessed them. What Jesus said suggests that he felt that the sense of wonder of a child was his passport to heaven. He was interested in the essence of human beings, and in children he saw a purity of spirit that had the possibility of eternal life.

Then Jesus talked about reconciliation and forgiveness because these subjects were very much on his mind. Typically, he begins: "If your brother sins against you go to him and show him his fault. But do it privately, just between yourselves. If he listens to you, you have won your brother back." If, however, the situation should escalate and ultimately your brother would not listen to reason, "treat him as though he was a foreigner or a tax collector." This last was a very interesting comment from Jesus, who was human and very provincial when he was caught off guard. But in fact, Jesus treated foreigners and tax collectors quite well. Jesus followed this up with the parable of the king who had to settle the accounts with his servants. One servant, who must have worked in a high official capacity, owed him the equivalent of millions of dollars. The king was in the process of selling this man and his family into slavery when he suddenly had a change of heart and restored the man to his position. Incredibly, this spared man turned and destroyed a lesser servant who owed him money. The king then sent this merciless official back to jail until he could repay the whole amount. "That is how my Father in heaven will treat you," Jesus said, "if you do not forgive your brother, every one of you, from the heart."

The Jewish Feast of Tabernacles was near, and Jesus' brothers urged him to go to Judea to attend the feast. Jesus shook them off and told them to go on to the feast by themselves, that the time was not right for him. But later, secretly, Jesus did go to Jerusalem. There was all of this controversy raging about Jesus, but nobody could find him there. And then when the feast was half over, Jesus went into the Temple and began teaching. The people did not immediately recognize him and they assumed he was some sort of prophet. Then some began to speculate that this might be the "Jesus" that the Pharisees were looking for.

"Isn't this the man they are trying to kill?" someone asked. "Look, he is talking in public, and nobody says anything against him! Can it be that the leaders really know that he is the Messiah? But when the Messiah comes, no one will know where he is from. And," they said confidently, "we all know where this man comes from."

Jesus had had enough of this nonsense and he answered them in a loud voice. "Do you really know me and know where I am from? But I have not come on my own. He who sent me, however, is true. You do not know him,

but I know him for I come from him and he sent me."
There was some sentiment in the group to arrest him but
nobody would lay the first hand on him. It didn't take
the Pharisees long to get information that Jesus was there
and when they were alerted, they sent guards to arrest
him. The guards found Jesus saying, "Whoever is thirsty
should come to me and drink. As the scripture says,
'Whoever believes in me, streams of living water will pour
out from his heart.'" The guards in the crowd argued
about who Jesus was, and some said, "He is the Messiah!"
But others said, "The Messiah will not come from
Galilee."

"Where is he?" the Pharisees asked when the guards
came back empty-handed. The guards shrugged their
shoulders and said, "Nobody has ever talked the way this
man does." "Did he fool you, too?" the Pharisees asked.
"Have you ever known one of our leaders or one Pharisee
to believe in him?" That was a sort of rhetorical question
that doesn't embarrass guards, but it did embarrass one
of the Pharisees, Nicodemus, who had known Jesus and
had been impressed by him. Trying to ease the situation
without exposing himself, Nicodemus said to the others,
"According to our Law we cannot condemn a man before
hearing him and finding out what he has done." "Well,"
they said, turning on Nicodemus, "are you from Galilee,
too? Study the scriptures and you will learn that no
prophet ever comes from Galilee." The priests had always
knocked Galilee as some sort of religious outback, yet
it was the most prosperous, populous, and lively of all
the regions of Palestine. Admittedly, by no stretch of the
imagination could Galilee be termed the most pious area.

Jesus knew he didn't come from the Bible Belt.

Everybody else went home, but Jesus went to the Mount of Olives to reflect and pray. Early the next morning he came back down to the Temple. A crowd gathered spontaneously and he sat down and began to teach. There was a sudden commotion. Jesus could see a group of lawyers and guards kicking and dragging a woman in his direction. The lawyers had had a bit of luck that morning and had gotten their hands on a woman who had been caught in the act of adultery.

"Teacher," one lawyer said to him with malicious glee, "this woman was caught in the very act of committing adultery. In our Law Moses gave a commandment that such a woman must be stoned to death. Now, what do you say?" Jesus had a good bit to say, but he held back for a moment and drew figures idly on the ground with his finger. He conjured over the trap set for him at the expense of this terrified and humiliated woman who huddled before him. It took no special divination to read the minds and the hearts of the men who were there ready to obey the Law with all the relish in the world. Jesus straightened up with clear, composed eyes and said to them, "Whichever one of you has committed no sin may throw the first stone at her." He spoke with intensity and as he spoke he looked right into the essential self of each man. Unmoved by the heat of their expectations, he put the hook of his question right into the heart of each man. "You?" he asked, and the question was flat and dry. "You? You? You?" One by one the men dropped their heads and walked away, the older ones first.

Jesus was left alone with the woman, still kneeling

where she had been thrown by one of the guards. He leaned down and spoke directly to her. "Where are they, woman? Is there no one left to condemn you?" "No one, Sir," she said. "Well, then," Jesus said, "I do not con- demn you either. You may leave but do not sin again." The woman must have looked at him as only a woman can. Her life had been spared, but the humiliation had been lifted, too. The power of this man had dissolved the horror behind the fear.

There had been no judgment, only illumination. The striking thing about Jesus' response to this hair-raising situation was his very matter-of-factness. He didn't moral- ize or justify, nor did he make any final judgment about the seriousness of the sin. He stepped away from the code and custom of the time, exacted justice from her accusers, and gave mercy to her.

Having dispatched with the first problem of the day, Jesus spoke with great feeling to the crowd in the Temple. And he talked right into the teeth of the Pharisees: "I am the light of the world. Whoever follows me will have the light of life and will never walk in darkness." "Ah," they said, "now you are testifying on your own behalf; what you say proves nothing." With hardened hearts they contested everything he said. This whole conversa- tion took place in the room in the Temple where the offering boxes were placed, so there was a tremendous amount of activity with people coming and going. But nobody arrested him.

Jesus leaned into them and coolly baited the officials. "You come from here below, but I come from above," Jesus told them. "You come from this world, but I do not come from this world. That is why I told you that you will die in your sins. And you will die in your sins if you do not believe that 'I am who I am.' "

The officials did not understand what Jesus was talking about, but many in the crowd who heard Jesus were strangely moved by him and found themselves believing in him. To them Jesus spoke very directly: "If you will obey my teaching you are really my disciples: you will know the truth and the truth will make you free." "We are the descendants of Abraham," they said, "we have never been anybody's slaves. What do you mean, then, by saying, 'You will be made free'?" Jesus said, "I tell you the truth, everyone who sins is a slave of sin." His listeners were perplexed because they could not under-stand what Jesus meant about sins and slavery. He tried again. "I know you are Abraham's descendants. Yet you are trying to kill me, because you will not accept my teaching. I talk about what my Father has shown me, but you do what your father has told you."

Finally, Jesus got into a fierce argument with the crowd when they accused him of having a demon and of being a Samaritan—both pretty serious charges from a Jewish point of view. Things got out of hand and he told them, "If anyone obeys my message, he will never die." They replied, "Now we know for sure that you have a demon. Who do you think you are?" Jesus' answers infuriated them, and they gathered stones to kill him. While they were organizing Jesus slipped away and left the Temple.

After conflict with local officials or a set-to with the crowd, Jesus almost always impulsively healed somebody; it was a way of completing something that was positive and useful without hassling with anybody. This time as he hurriedly left the Temple his attention was caught by a man who had been born blind. "Teacher," the disciples asked, "whose sin was it that caused him to be born blind? His own, or his parents' sin?" Jesus answered them forcefully: "His blindness has nothing to do with his sins or his parents' sins. He is blind so that God's power might be seen at work in him." Then Jesus spat on the ground and made some mud with the spittle; he put the mud on the man's eyes and told him, "Go wash your face in the Pool of Siloam." The man went and washed his face, and came back seeing.

This miracle caused great controversy. The healed man said clearly what had happened to him, but the Pharisees argued, "The man who did this cannot be from God because he does not obey the sabbath law." They had done original research to prove that the cure took place on the sabbath. But there was a considerable division about this because some people wanted to know how a sinner could do such mighty works. So the Pharisees began to claim that the man had not been blind in the first place. They called his parents: "Is this your son? Do you say that he was born blind? Well, how is it that he can see now?"

The conversation that follows is really marvelous because it is an exercise in the denial of reality, the sort of rigamarole that bureaucracy is famous for throughout the ages. The parents were dismayed and very wary of the Pharisees, so they answered, "We know that he is our son, and we know that he was born blind, but we do not know how it is that he is now able to see, nor do we know who opened his eyes. Ask him; he is old enough, and he can answer for himself!"

The Pharisees rousted up the recovered blind man who could see like an eagle now, and began interrogating him all over again. "Promise before God that you will tell the truth! We know that this man is a sinner." "I don't know if he is a sinner or not," the man replied. "One thing I do know: I was blind and now I see." "How did he open your eyes?" the Pharisees asked. "I already told you," he answered. "And you would not listen. Why do you want to hear it again? Maybe you, too, would like to be his disciples?"

They cursed him, and said, "You are that fellow's disciple; we are Moses' disciples. We know that God spoke to Moses; as for that fellow, we do not even know where he comes from!" "What a strange thing this is!" the man said, looking about him with great interest. "You do not know where he comes from, but he opened my eyes! We know that God does not listen to sinners; he does listen to people who respect him and do what he wants them to do. Since the beginning of the world it has never been heard of that someone opened the eyes of a blind man; unless this man comes from God, he would not be able to do such a thing." "You were born in sin— and you are trying to teach us?" they shouted at him. And then they threw him out of the Temple. So this blessed man ended up being punished for his miraculous cure.

Later Jesus met the man again and identified himself, and the man believed and knelt down before him. Jesus said to the man and to the group around him, including some lawyers and Pharisees, "I came to this world to judge so that the blind should see, and those who see should become blind." One of the Pharisees muttered, "You don't mean that we are blind, too?" And Jesus answered, "If you were blind then you would not be guilty; but since you say, 'We can see', that means you are still guilty."

Jesus launched another attack on the Pharisees and scribes. The good shepherd, Jesus said, is willing to die for the sheep. The hired man who is not a shepherd and does not own the sheep leaves them as soon as he sees a wolf coming. As Jesus talked about being willing to die for his sheep, the Jews were perplexed. Some were sure that he was crazy, but others admitted that they could not fathom how a man with a demon could talk as Jesus talked. Nor could they explain how any madman could open the eyes of a blind man.

It was getting pretty nervewracking to disprove all of Jesus' cures. They were coming thick and fast, and many of the beneficiaries were standing around in hearty shape, available to discuss their medical histories and very cheer-ful about their good fortunes. It would be easy to make a case against men who put people's eyes out, or maimed or killed them, but it was indeed awkward to try to charge successful faith healers with technical infractions of the law such as violating the sabbath. The opposition had to snatch at straws and they concentrated on the issue of blasphemy. Desperately and bitterly, they condemned Jesus for insulting God, even for playing God.

Winter had come and Jesus was walking in the portico of Solomon in the Temple. It was the Feast of the Dedication at Jerusalem, and Jesus had raised the sort of questions in the minds of the religious community that could not be stilled. At the moment Jesus was the most newsworthy personality in Palestine, and an instant press conference wherever he appeared. Some officials caught sight of him that afternoon and swarmed around.

"How long are you going to keep us in suspense?" they asked. "Tell us the plain truth: are you the Messiah?" Jesus said, "I have already told you, but you would not believe me. The works I do by my Father's authority speak on my behalf; but you will not believe because you are not my sheep. My sheep listen to my voice; I know them, and they follow me. I give them eternal life, and they shall never die; no one can snatch them away from me. What my Father has given me is greater than all, and no one can snatch them away from the Father's care. The Father and I are one."

Jesus was still talking in that elliptical way that nourished the believers but did not give the hostile listeners the evidence to move in on him. He knew that he was fair game, that the Pharisees had given their tacit approval for him to be destroyed, but had made no overt signal. It was cat and mouse, and Jesus had to play it carefully because, as he said, "The time was not right yet."

The officials were infuriated by what he said about himself, but they were confused by his acts. He had thrown sand in their eyes. His enemies were violent, temperamental human beings with great capability for easy violence, but Jesus was bleeding it off, bit by bit, without letting it explode. Several men took up stones to throw at him but Jesus said quickly, "I have done many good works before you; for which of these do you stone me?" His would-be assailants, still clutching their stones, said, "We do not want to stone you because of any good works, but because of the way in which you insult God. You are only a man, and you are trying to make yourself God!"

Jesus answered quick as a flash: "It is written in your own Law that God said, 'You are Gods.' We know that what the scripture says is true forever; and he called them Gods, those people to whom God's message was given. As for me, the Father chose me and sent me into the world. How, then, can you say that I insult God because I said that I am the Son of God?"

This was an extraordinary comment which revealed the way he saw himself in relation to God. In a sense it was a pioneering effort to cast man's relationship to God in a different perspective. But it was more than the angry men could stand and they summoned guards to arrest Jesus. Again he slipped away and this time he put some distance between himself and the Temple because it was obvious that there was an overwhelming sentiment to place him under arrest. Once they grabbed him, it would be hard for them to let him go. Jesus' masterly instinct for survival took over because he knew it was not time for him to give himself up.

He walked swiftly out of Jerusalem and started hiking along familiar trails toward the spot where his cousin John had baptized him. The scene had remained in his mind with burning clarity—there had not been any clearer fork in the road. It was the first time in his life that he had felt directly connected to God. This experience was something that had helped him make sense out of everything that had happened since.

He settled down in the crook of the river, and the support that he drew from being in that place heartened him so that he became completely at ease. A reaffirmation of his mission flowed into him and Jesus stored up vitality and composure for the days ahead. As he was ready to move on, an urgent message came to him from Bethany. Mary and Martha had sent one fateful bit of information about their brother: "Lord, your dear friend Lazarus is sick." The sisters had also endeared themselves to Jesus through their commitment to him, and Jesus knew that he would have to go to Bethany. But in his mind there was no rush. In two days Jesus broke camp on the Jordan and was on his way.

Since Bethany was only a few miles from Jerusalem, Jesus' disciples were wary about his going back. "Teacher," they said, "just a short time ago the Jews wanted to stone you; and you plan to go back there?" Jesus explained that "our friend Lazarus has fallen asleep, but I will go wake him." The disciples didn't understand and they thought that in those parlous times that was an unnecessary effort to make. "If he is asleep, Lord, he will get well," they said. So Jesus said, "Now listen, Lazarus is dead; but for your sake I am glad that I was not with him, so you will believe. Let us go to him."

When they got to Bethany, they found that Lazarus was not only dead—he had been buried for four days. A great traffic of people was coming to and from Jerusalem to comfort Mary and Martha. When Martha heard that Jesus was coming along the road, she went out to meet him, but Mary stayed at home to take care of the guests and run the house. Martha's first words to Jesus after her greeting were a sorrowful, "If you had been here, Lord, my brother would not have died! But, I know that even now God will give you whatever you ask of him." This broad hint was not lost on Jesus. "Your brother will be raised to life," Jesus told her. Martha replied that she was sure that Lazarus would be raised to life on the great day of judgment. Jesus said, "I am the resurrection and the life. Whoever believes in me will live, even though he dies, and whoever lives and believes in me will never die. Do you believe this?" "Yes, Lord," she answered. "I do believe that you are the Messiah, the Son of God, who was to come into the world."

After this remarkable exchange, Martha rushed back to the house and called her sister Mary. Mary hurried out and found Jesus in almost the same spot where Martha had first seen him. The group around Martha and Mary wept bitterly as the impact of Lazarus' death hit them again. Jesus was touched by them and he asked, "Where have you buried him?" "Come and see, Lord," they said. They led him along. Jesus was so moved that he wept on the way to the tomb.

The friends who had come with Mary from the house noted with satisfaction that he was weeping. "See how much Jesus loved him." After all he was a celebrity and it was very flattering to have him join in their grief and become one with them. They began to recount his miracles. Could he not have kept Lazarus from dying?

When they got to the tomb, Jesus stood looking at the stone that had been rolled against the cave in the hillside

that held Lazarus' body. He ordered them to take the
stone away. "But Lord," Martha replied, "there will be
a bad smell, he has been buried for four days." Jesus
shrugged it off. The men in the group proceeded to roll
the stone away. Jesus looked up and said for all to hear,
"I thank you, Father, that you listen to me. I know that
you always listen to me, but I say this because of the
people here, so they will believe that you sent me." Then
he called out in a loud voice, "Lazarus, come out." The
dead man did come out, with his hands and feet still
wrapped in graveclothes, and a cloth around his face.
"Untie him," Jesus ordered, "and let him go."

Jesus is moving ahead of fast-breaking events, and there
is a sense of urgency in everything he does. He increased
the size of his staff and sent disciples ahead of him, two
by two, as advance men. No one with second thoughts
was admitted to the team. As the group passed through a
small village in Judea, one man came forward and said to
Jesus, "Master, I will follow you wherever you go."
Jesus said to him, "Foxes have holes; and the birds of the
air have nests; but the Son of man has nowhere to lay
his head." It was a way of saying that this was going to
be a hardrock campaign and there would be no relief,
even for the leader. Another man offered to join the
group and was accepted. But then he had an afterthought:
"Lord, let me first go and bury my father." He got a
quick answer. "Leave the dead to bury their own dead.
You go and preach the kingdom of God." "I will follow
you, Sir," still another man said. "But first let me go and
say good-by to my family." Jesus looked him over and
said, "Anyone who starts to plow and then keeps looking

back is of no use for the kingdom of God."

This was a harsh ruling, but Jesus knew that a man who had to go back home again could never leave his home behind. There could be no looking back for this small band: they would need all of their possible concentration of mind and heart to capture the future. There could be no allowance for family ties; no retreat; no quarter for division of love or loyalty.

In all Jesus appointed about seventy two disciples. They were single-minded; they had resolve; they had an instinct for truth beyond their understanding. Jesus gave explicit marching orders. He gave them the same sort of warnings and admonitions he had given the twelve when he sent them out on their own.

The seventy-two made their appointed rounds and returned truly amazed with themselves. "Lord," they said, "even the demons obeyed us when we commanded them in your name." When they told him this, Jesus was enormously encouraged, and cried, "I saw Satan fall like lightning from heaven. Listen, I have given you authority, so that you could walk on snakes and scorpions and nothing will hurt you. But don't be glad because the evil spirits obey you; rather be glad because your names are written in heaven."

This last view is consistent with Jesus' whole attitude toward miracles. He always seems diffident, almost embarrassed with the dramatic effect of miracles. He would not perform them on demand or in an atmosphere of skepticism or hostility. His miracles were practical, useful, humane—the power was not self-originating and the expression was not self-glorifying. The magician uses his magic to create believers, but Jesus introduced believers to mystical powers that he always attributed to God.

In his parables Jesus begins to broaden the respon-sibility of man and to change the definition of neighbor. A lawyer jousting with Jesus asks him, "What shall I do to receive eternal life, Teacher?" He got the question right back. "What do the Scriptures say? How do you interpret them?" The lawyer said, "You must love the Lord your God with all your heart, and with all your soul, and with all your strength, and with all your mind; and you must love your neighbor as yourself." "Your answer is correct," Jesus replied. "Do this and you will live." It was a classical answer and Jesus had not been trapped into anything that could be called blasphemy. The lawyer made another stab.

"Who is my neighbor?" he asked Jesus. Jesus answered by telling him the famous story of the Good Samaritan. The route from Jerusalem to Jericho was a very familiar road that both Jesus and the lawyer had traveled many times. And any man going that way might expect to run across a priest, a Levite, and a Samaritan. After Jesus had told the lawyer about the traveler who was attacked by robbers and then ignored by the priest and the Levite before the Samaritan rescued him, he asked the lawyer, "Which one of these three seems to you to have been a neighbor to the man attacked by the robbers?" "The one who was kind to him," the lawyer said, unable to bring himself to say "Samaritan." "You go, then, and do the same," Jesus told him. The lawyer was furious, for he had answered both of his questions himself. He had been instructed like a helpless student. And disputation was supposed to be *his* game.

A rich man who was a Jewish leader overtook Jesus in the countryside, and came running up to him. He knelt down reverently and said, "What must I do to receive eternal life?" Jesus told him, "You know the command- ments." "Ever since I was young I have obeyed all these commandments," the man said. With love in his eyes Jesus looked straight at him. "You need only one thing. Go and sell all you have and give the money to the poor, and you will have riches in heaven; then come and follow me." When the man heard this gloom spread over his face and he went away because he was very rich.

Jesus looked round at his followers and said to them as they rested at the top of the hill, "How hard it will be for rich men to enter the kingdom of God." His listeners were shocked but Jesus expanded the theme: "It is much harder for a rich man to enter the kingdom of God than for a camel to go through the eye of a needle." "Who, then, can be saved?" one listener cried. Jesus looked di- rectly at him and answered, "This is impossible for men, but not for God; everything is possible for God." Peter reminded Jesus that they had in fact left their homes to follow him. And Jesus responded that they would be more than repaid for their decision—enough to more than repay for relatives, loved ones, homes and jobs.

Jesus did not mean that there was anything wrong with having your heart's desire, even if that meant riches. What he did require was that all the things of this earthly kingdom must be subordinated to the kingdom of God.

Possessions were not wrong but they were dangerous. The rich man who turned away was a prisoner of things. He was ingrained with the habit of wanting, getting, having. It was a sort of idolatry. Rich men don't belong to themselves, they belong to their things. Thus this young man who could have been a man for all ages decided not to wager what he had on any shaky possibility. He just happened to guess wrong. The disciples were very much affected by this episode. By and large they were not rich and they had had their regrets about not acquiring wealth. Now they were told that this was in truth an advantage. Wonder of wonders, longing for riches was not nearly so bad as having them. And not longing for them was best of all.

One day on the road, Jesus was praying. When he finished, one of the group said to him, "Lord, teach us to pray, just as John the baptizer taught his disciples." And this is the prayer Jesus taught them: "Father, thy name be hallowed; thy kingdom come. Give us each day our daily bread. And forgive us our sins, for we too forgive all who have done us wrong. And do not bring us to the test. But save us from the evil one." This prayer is striking for its plainness and for its pious but informal tone with God. It is enormously personal, obviously meant to be prayed in private and not overheard. Jesus had spoken very harshly about showing off with public displays of religion. He was contemptuous of wordy prayers—as he said, "God already knows what you want."

Jesus was talking to people who had been taught to be terrified of God and who had a very formal relationship with him. "Would any one of your fathers give his son a snake when he asks for fish?" Jesus asked. "Or would you give him a scorpion when he asks for an egg? As bad as you are, you know how to give good things to your children. How much more, then, the Father in heaven will give the Holy Spirit to those who ask him." The mentality that Jesus was working on had been locked into a wrathful and wholly terrifying God whose attention you did not want to invoke unnecessarily. Against this view Jesus taught about God who was like a father, who kept track of you, who cared for and listened to you. This was a highly portable God that could be introduced to the gentiles, and that could be called upon for help at every turn in the ominous days ahead.

Another time Jesus was addressing a huge crowd and he talked to them about many things in rich symbolic language that they understood immediately on one level and then again, later, in a deeper way. The people responded to him warmly and shouted many questions at him. One man asked a practical question and soon everybody was besieging Jesus about their personal problems. From out of the crowd a voice said, "Teacher, tell my brother to divide with me the property our father left us." Jesus answered him, "Man, who gave me the right to judge or divide the property between you two?" Then Jesus tore into the group as if he knew that greed was a special weakness in the minds and hearts before him. "Watch out and guard yourselves from any kind of greed; for a man's true life is not made up of the things he owns, no matter how rich he may be."

He went on to tell them a story about a rich man who kept building bigger and bigger barns to hold his crops and goods, and just as he was settling back to take life easy, he heard from God. "You fool," God said, "this very night you will have to give up your life; then who will get all these things you have kept for yourself?" Then he talked about faithful and unfaithful servants, and the readiness of the master, God, to close the great account book of life. His concept of what would happen to the servant who "was not ready" or the servant who "was drunk and abusing the other servants" was sufficiently dire to give us an idea of what Jesus thought to be reason- able justice. "The master will cut him to pieces, and make him share the fate of the disobedient," he said.

The truth of the matter is that in our light Jesus could be a very fierce character. This is in terms of the attitudes of the man and the accepted levels of brutality and violence of his time. Yet against his literal toughness and physical composure, he also expressed an overflowing humanity and a gentleness with women and children. We see this dramatic opposition again and again. There is no soft core to this man.

He makes it perfectly clear that the alternatives for man are unquenchable fire on the one hand and eternal life on the other. Jesus regards both possibilities very calmly with no waffling of the nerves when he says, "You will have this, and *you* will have that." Once he said, "I came to set the earth on fire, and how I wish it were already kindled. I have a baptism to receive, and how dis- tressed I am until it is over. Do you suppose that I came to bring peace to the world? Not peace, I tell you, but division."

There were bad vibrations in Jesus' group at this time

because of rumors about plots against Jesus, and his disciples were filled with alarm. It was a wearying and terrifying ritual, but Jesus had to keep telling his staff about what was going to happen to him. "Look, we are going up to Jerusalem where the Son of Man will be handed over to the chief priests and the teachers of the Law. They will condemn him to death and then hand him over to the gentiles. These will make fun of him, spit on him, whip him, and kill him. And after three days he will be raised to life." They just could not grasp what he was saying. But if the disciples could not understand the destiny of Jesus, they were even less able to understand how the Kingdom stood in relation to that fate.

The great proof of this was the pitch that James and John, sons of Zebedee, made to Jesus. "When you sit on your throne in the glorious Kingdom, we want you to let us sit with you, one at your right and one at your left." Jesus came back at them very quickly. "You don't know what you are asking for. Can you drink the cup that I must drink and be baptized in the way I must be baptized?" "We can," they answered. And Jesus said, "You will indeed drink the cup I must drink and be baptized in the way I must be baptized, but I do not have the right to choose who will sit at my right and my left. It is God who will give these places to those for whom he had prepared them."

The other disciples were bitterly angry with James and John for making this request. So Jesus called them all together and gave them a lecture on their relationship to each other. "The one who is great in my Kingdom is the one who will be servant to the others. So if any one of you here wants to be first, he must be the servant of all the others."

Jesus was on his way to Jerusalem when he came to Jericho and found that a great crowd of people awaited him. On the edge of the town he passed by a blind beggar, Bartimaeus, the son of Timaeus, who was sitting on the shoulder of the road. Bartimaeus wanted to know what was going on, since he was choking to death on the dust kicked up by the crowd. A man next to him said that Jesus of Nazareth was going by. Bartimaeus immediately began to shout, "Jesus! Son of David! Have mercy on me!" He was being a pest and he was not a terribly popular blind man anyhow, so the group around Jesus scolded him and told him to be quiet. But Jesus heard his voice and called to him. Bartimaeus threw off his cloak and sprang in the direction of Jesus' voice. "What do you want me to do for you?" Jesus asked. Bartimaeus said, "Teacher, I want to see again." "Go," Jesus told him, "your faith has made you well."

The fact that Jesus was controversial did not make him any less popular. The good news seemed to be more contagious all the time, and Jesus was changing the lives of the people he came in contact with. In Jericho, Jesus found the roadway packed with people seven deep like a crowd watching a parade. Lost in the mob was a man named Zacchaeus, a very rich chief tax collector. In addition to having a very undesirable professional reputation, Zacchaeus had the burden of being virtually a midget. He could not see Jesus, and he was frantic to get a glimpse of him, so Zacchaeus climbed a sycamore tree and scampered out on the limb just as Jesus came that way.

To Zacchaeus' utter confoundment, Jesus looked up at him and said, "Hurry down, Zacchaeus, for I must stay in your house today." Zacchaeus hurried down joyfully as the crowd grumbled that Jesus should choose to be the guest of such an unsavory man. The tax collector was aware of the reaction and quickly tried to justify Jesus' gesture by standing up as tall as he could and saying, "Listen, I will give half my belongings to the poor; and if I have cheated anyone, I will pay him back four times as much." Jesus said to him, "Salvation has come to this house today; this man, also, is a descendant of Abraham. For the Son of man came to seek and to save the lost."

It was the greatest compliment that Zacchaeus could have been given and he was beside himself with delight.

Now the government officials had been getting full reports from the spies who had been gathering evidence against Jesus. Word had long since come to them about Lazarus and his rescue from death at the hand of Jesus after being buried for four days. When they could not break down these stories, they planned how they might kill Lazarus because he was such persuasive evidence that Jesus had the power of God working through him. And there were many other reports of cures and miracles, and of the crowds that followed Jesus wherever he went. Most disturbing were the accounts of the number of con' verts (which the Pharisees discounted) and the repeated reports that Jesus could have as many disciples as he wanted, but that he set strict requirements and took only a few.

All of the top officials came into a council meeting to discuss what should be done. The Pharisees and the chief priests asked each other, "What shall we do? All the mighty works this man is doing! If we let him go on in this way everyone will believe in him, and the Roman authorities will take action and destroy the Temple and our whole nation." A man named Caiaphas, who was High Priest that year, said, "Don't you realize it would be better for one man to die rather than for the whole nation to be destroyed?" From that day on, the authorities made plans to kill Jesus. Friends from the council got word to the disciples and Jesus did not travel openly in Judea, but left and went into a place near the desert, to a town named Ephraim, where he stayed with his companions.

But the Jewish Feast of Passover was near, and many people were going from the country to Jerusalem to perform the ceremony of purification before the Feast. They were looking for Jesus and as they gathered in the Temple they asked one another, "What do you think? Surely he will not come to the Feast, will he?"

⟦ FAILURE ⟧

JESUS DECIDED that it was time for him to take his company into Jerusalem. He walked at the head of the column, and as they came near Bethphage and Bethany, at the Mount of Olives, Jesus sent two assistants ahead with special instructions.

"Go to the village there ahead of you; as you go in, you will find a colt tied up that has never been ridden. Untie it and bring it here. If someone asks you, 'Why are you untying it?' tell him, 'The Master needs it.' "

The two hurried along, nervous about the prospect of going to the Temple in Jerusalem, and therefore glad to have a diversionary job to do. They found everything just as Jesus had said. The owner did ask them what they were doing and they told him what they were instructed to say, and he gave his permission by a wordless nod of his head. They took the colt to Jesus, threw their cloaks over the animal, and he got on.

As he rode down the Mount of Olives, others spread their cloaks on the road before the colt. And when he came near Jerusalem on the lower slope of the Mount of

Olives, a large crowd of his disciples began to thank God and praise him in loud voices for all the great things they had seen. "Hosanna to the Son of David! Blessed is he who comes in the name of the Lord. Peace in heaven, and glory to God!" The joyfulness of the parade annoyed some Pharisees who were also making their way to Jerusalem, and they complained to Jesus. "Teacher," they said, "command your disciples to be quiet." Jesus answered, "If they keep quiet, I tell you, the stones themselves will shout."

When Jesus came closer to the city and could see all of Jerusalem before him, he wept over it: "If you only knew today what is needed for peace. And now you cannot see it. For the days will come upon you when your enemies will surround you with barricades, blockade you, and close in on you from every side. They will completely destroy you and the people within your walls; not a single stone will they leave in its place, because you did not recognize the time when God came to save you!" The parade lasted most of the day as it wound its way into Jerusalem and to the Temple. So Jesus walked around the Temple and looked the situation over, and then returned to Bethany with his twelve closest disciples.

The next morning the whole group returned to Jerusalem, and as Jesus walked along he was overtaken with a fierce hunger. Looking ahead he saw a fig tree by the side of the road that gave him a vision of delicious ripe figs for breakfast. When he got to the tree he found nothing on it but leaves—not a fig. In an angry morning temper he withered it. "You will never again bear fruit!" he said to the tree. Before the widening eyes of the disciples, it dried up on the spot. "How did the fig tree dry up so quickly?" they asked. "Remember this," Jesus told them. "If you believe, and do not doubt, you will be able to do what I have done to this fig tree; not only this, you will even be able to say to this hill, 'Get up and throw yourself in the sea,' and it will. If you believe, you will receive whatever you ask for in prayer."

It is likely that Jesus produced this frivolous, bedazzling little miracle as pure bad temper and fireworks. The re-deeming social value seems to have been an afterthought. It is unlike Jesus who, as a miracle worker, had none of the magic man in his makeup. To make the story more interesting, Mark reports that the reason the tree didn't have figs was that it wasn't the season for figs. Whatever the case, Jesus was tense, his temper was wearing thin, and the disciples after this were probably a little quicker about getting breakfast ready.

When the group got down to the Temple, Jesus' mood had not improved a bit. He went into the great inner room and with an angry roar began driving out all the merchants. He overturned the tables of the money-changers and the stools of the pigeon sellers. Amidst the clanking of change on the floor and the flurry of escaping pigeons, Jesus shouted after the dismayed tradesmen: "It is written in the scriptures that God said, 'My house will be called a house of prayer,' but you are making it a hide-out for thieves!" Jesus really tore the place up.

The blind and the crippled swarmed to Jesus in the Temple as they had in the cities, in the fields, and on the shores of the Sea of Galilee. The mob scene took place all over the Pharisees and the lawyers, and Jesus completely took the play away from them. He began to heal the lepers, open the eyes of the blind, and make the deaf hear—pandemonium reigned. Jesus was doing a brisker business than all of the money-changers and the pigeon sellers together.

A number of children were crying and shouting in the Temple, "Praise to David's Son." The chief priests and the teachers of the Law were indignant and they screamed at Jesus, "Do you hear what they are saying?" "Indeed I do," Jesus said. Then he asked mockingly, "Haven't you ever read the scripture that says, 'You have trained children and babies to offer perfect praise'?" These haughty scholars of the scriptures were flabbergasted by the impudence and aptness of Jesus' comment, and by the time they had recovered their wits he was gone. Jesus rejoined his disciples and again they went to Bethany to spend the night.

In bureaucratic establishments the operative question is always "by what authority?" Not, what is this miracle you are performing, but, who told you you could perform a miracle on company time? "What right do you have to do these things?" This question put by leading government officials was Jesus' introduction to the Temple the next day. So Jesus took them over the jumps with a rapid question that was of great interest to the mob in the room where he was sparring with his adversaries.

"Now let me ask you a question," Jesus said. "Tell me, did John's right to baptize come from God or from man?" They started to argue among themselves. "What shall we say? If we say 'from God,' he will say, 'Why, then, did you not believe John?' But if we say 'from man,' this whole crowd here will stone us because they are convinced John was a prophet." So they answered, "We don't know where it came from." Jesus said to them, "Neither will I tell you, then, by what right I do these things."

Jesus began to tell parables, the first of which was bitter and hard, and reflected his feelings toward the officials of Jerusalem. It was a story of a man who planted a vineyard and rented it out to tenants and then left home for a long time. He sent slaves to collect his share of the harvest, and then he sent his own son, and all of them were beaten, but the son was both beaten and killed. Obviously God had planted the vineyard and the Pharisees could take it from there. "What, then, will the owner of the vineyard do to the tenants?" Jesus answered his own question, "He will come and kill those men, and turn over the vineyard to other tenants."

"Surely not," one listener said. Jesus looked at him and said, "What, then, does this scripture mean? 'The stone which the builders rejected as worthless turned out to be the most important stone.' Everyone who falls on that stone will be cut to pieces; if the stone falls on someone, it will crush him to dust." Jesus wanted to make abso- lutely certain that they understood that God was playing for keeps, just as they were. It was time to get the amateurs out of the bidding, and to make it clear to the people just exactly what the opposition was. The priests and lawyers wanted to arrest Jesus on the spot because they under- stood what he was saying, but they were afraid of the people. So they waited and watched for the right time.

Some Pharisees, in the meantime, got into an uneasy

combine with Herod's men, and they conjured together as to how they could trap Jesus. They came to him with a sticky line. "Teacher," they said, "we know that what you say and teach is right. We know that you pay no attention to what a man seems to be, but teach the truth about God's will for man. Tell us, then, what do you think? Is it against our Law to pay taxes to the Roman emperor or not?" Jesus saw the trap without much difficulty. "Show me the coin to pay the tax." They brought him a coin. "Whose face and name are these?" "The Emperor's," they answered. "Well, then, pay to the Emperor what belongs to him, and pay to God what belongs to God." When they heard this they knew he had the best of them, and they went away.

Everybody was suffering under the Roman tax, and the Jews were in a constant state of hysteria about it. Taking this loaded question, Jesus very crisply separated the grievance of the day from eternal obligation. What Jesus was asking was, "Who mints these coins?" And implicitly he was asking, "What is God's coin?—You." His implication that everything belonged to God was enough to get the Pharisees off his back that day, and the simple lesson of the inevitability of taxes was a reflection of the very practical nature of Jesus—he was not going to tilt against taxes.

Next, the Sadducees made their run at Jesus. As a group they were more conservative than the Pharisees, and they did not believe in life after death or in angels. They said to Jesus that Moses taught that if a childless man were to die, his brother should marry the widow so that they could have children for the dead man. Consider, then, the following case, they said. Suppose there were seven brothers in a village. Each in turn married and died without having children, leaving the widow to his next oldest brother. Finally all seven had died in the same situation, and last of all, the woman herself died. And then came the question: "Now, when the dead are raised to life, whose wife will she be? All of them had married her!"

It was a vulgar question but it raised real problems that everybody thought about. What was it going to be like in heaven? The Sadducees who didn't believe in heaven at all were delighted to make it an illogical and inhospitable place. There was pure malice in the ques' tion, but Jesus answered it seriously. "How wrong you are! And do you know why? It is because you don't know the scriptures or God's power. But when the dead are raised to life they will be like the angels in heaven, and men and women will not marry. Now, about the dead being raised: haven't you ever read in the Book of Moses the passage about the burning bush? For there it is written that God said to Moses, 'I am the God of Abraham, the God of Isaac, and the God of Jacob.' That means that he is the God of the living, not the dead. You are completely wrong."

When the Pharisees heard that Jesus had silenced the Sadducees, they came forward with a question of their own. One of the lawyers asked Jesus which command' ment was the most important. This is the most important one," Jesus said. "Hear, Israel! The Lord our God is the only Lord. You must love the Lord your God with all your heart, and with all your soul, and with all your

mind, and with all your strength.' The second most important commandment is this: 'You must love your
neighbor as yourself.' There is no other commandment
more important than these two."

Sometimes Jesus knocked the opposition out and won
them over despite themselves. The lawyer exclaimed,
"Well done, Teacher!" He repeated what Jesus had
said, agreeing completely, and even volunteered, "It is
much better to obey these two commandments than to
bring animals to be burned on the alter and offer other
sacrifices to God." Jesus told him, "You are not far from
the kingdom of God." It is very important to understand
Jesus' attitude toward the kingdom; the kingdom was a
movable kingdom in which anyone could be included,
and for Jesus it was very much a "kingdom now."

The hypocrisy of the Jewish leaders infuriated Jesus.
He knew they loved the best seats at dinner, and reserved
seats in the meetinghouses. They loved titles, and demanded that they be treated with respect in the marketplace. "They fix up heavy loads and tie them on men's
backs, yet they aren't willing even to lift a finger to help
them carry those loads. They do everything just so people will see them."

His anger on this day knew no bounds. "How terrible
for you teachers of the Law and Pharisees! Impostors!
You lock the door to the kingdom of heaven in men's
faces but you yourselves will not go in, and neither will
you let people in who are trying to go in. You take advantage of widows and rob them of their homes, and
then make a show of saying long prayers. You sail the
seas and cross whole countries to win one convert; and

when you succeed, you make him twice as deserving of
going to hell as you yourselves are! You give to God
one tenth even of the seasoning herbs such as mint, dill,
and cumin, but you neglect to obey the really important teachings of the Law such as justice and mercy and
honesty."

Jesus challenges them to go ahead and do what he
knows they are going to do—put 'him to death. In the
face of the crowd, he puts himself into the tradition of
those tormented and destroyed by the Pharisees and the
teachers of the Law. His freedom from moment to moment depends on his masterly management of the crowd,
for he is playing on the officials' fear of explosive riot-
ing. That, of course, would bring Romans down on all
their backs.

What the officials did not know was that Jesus himself would not accept any kind of political or military
leadership; he was not going to fulfill the prophecy in
the sense that it had been interpreted. So, in that moment in the Temple he was maintaining a precarious
balance. It was the beginning of some sort of momentous
countdown.

Finally, pity and irony overwhelmed the anger in his
mind, and Jesus is appalled by the revelation of the agony
and desolation the Jews have brought up themselves.
And would bring. "O Jerusalem, Jerusalem," he cried,
"you kill the prophets and stone the messengers God
has sent you! How many times have I wanted to put
my arms around all your people, just as a hen gathers
her chicks under her wings, but you would not let me.
Now your home will be completely forsaken. From now

on you will never see me again, I tell you, until you say,
'God bless him who comes in the name of the Lord."

Jesus turned impulsively to leave the Temple, his path
taking him past people putting money in the offering
boxes. Among the rich people putting in large sums of
money, he saw a poor widow who gave two copper coins,
which together were worth a penny. From the woman's
dress he knew the style of her life and the privation she
was forced to endure, and he could guess how little she
had to spend on herself. "Truly," he said, "this poor
widow has put in more than all of the others." This interpretation was as extraordinary in the first century as
it is now. You can't buy God. There is instant parity
between the poor man and the rich man in the eyes of
God, and striking equity in the good news—along with
the meek and pure in heart, the poor have an inside
track.

As they left the Temple, the disciples gaped at the
massiveness and grandeur of the building. They were as
fascinated as a bunch of tourists. "Looked at these wonderful stones, and these great buildings," one said. But Jesus
had been drawn into a much more serious frame of mind.
"Yes," he said, "you may well look at all these buildings.
I tell you this: not a single stone here will be left in its
place; every one of them will be thrown down."

It was inconceivable to the disciples that the Temple
would be destroyed, or that their whole life with Jesus
would rapidly come to an end. As they discussed this
on the Mount of Olives in their private gathering place,
one put the question to Jesus directly. "Tell us when
all this will be," he asked, "and what will happen to

show that it is the time for your coming and the end of the age." Jesus warned him, "Watch out, and do not let anyone fool you. Many men will come in my name, saying, 'I am the Messiah,' and they will fool many people. And you will hear of wars and rumors of wars, but listen—do not be troubled. For all these things are like the first pains of childbirth."

Looking directly at his disciples and tying them into his future, Jesus said, "Then men will arrest you and hand you over to be punished, and you will be put to death. All mankind will hate you because of me. Many will give up their faith at that time. They will betray each other and hate each other. Then many false prophets will appear and fool many people. Such will be the spread of evil, and many people's love will grow cold. But the person who holds out to the end will be saved. And this good news about the kingdom will be preached through all the world, for a witness to all mankind—and then will come the end."

Jesus is preconditioning his disciples for the privations that lie ahead and for the terrible fate that awaits many of them personally, but he is doing more than that. He is doing them the honor of telling them the eternal importance of their roles; he is celebrating the fact that this tiny group is being entrusted with a message that could save mankind.

They are the messengers; they have the good news; and they must get through to the future.

The panoramic picture which Jesus created was that of a civilization falling to pieces. He was explicit in his prediction of the fall of Jerusalem. To his followers' mind, anything as cataclysmic as the destruction of Jerusalem was inextricably tied to the fate of all mankind. All the threads of Judaism were gathered up in a tangible way in Jerusalem and particularly in the literal physical expression of the Temple. Jesus' awful forecast reached far beyond the Holy City. He described stars falling from the heavens, the earth rent with earthquakes and tidal waves, the sun darkening, and lightning scorching the sky from east to west. The judgment of man would follow and then the Son of Man would return with power and glory.

Jesus told a hard truth in a harsh parable: "When the Son of Man comes in his glory, and all the angels with him, he will sit on his royal throne, and all the earth's people will be gathered before him. Then he will divide them into two groups, just as the shepherd separates the sheep from the goats: he will put the sheep at his right and the goats at his left. Then the king will say to the people on his right: 'You who are blessed by my Father: come and receive the kingdom which has been prepared for you ever since the creation of the world. I was hungry and you fed me, thirsty and you gave me drink; I was a stranger and you received me in your homes, naked and you clothed me; I was sick and you took care of me, in prison and you visited me.' The righteous will then answer him: 'When, Lord, did we ever see you hungry and feed you, or thirsty and give you drink? When did we ever see you a stranger and welcome you in our homes, or naked and clothe you? When did we ever see you sick or in prison, and visit you?' The king will answer back, 'I tell you, indeed, whenever you did this for one of these poorest brothers of mine, you did it for me!' "

This was the whole story of who would get into the Kingdom and it was devastating because those who had been absolutely certain of making it were out, and those who could not possibly justify being elected to it were in. It was a real cold-turkey parable that did nothing to ease the pain of giving up self-deception and accepting the truth.

In many such stories Jesus tried to tell his followers to be attentive, to be prepared when God came and stood at the gate. "Watch yourselves. Don't let yourselves become occupied with too much feasting and strong drink, and the worries of this life, for that Day may come on you suddenly like a snare for all who dwell upon the face of the whole earth." There was not going to be any general admission to the kingdom. There would be no way to get in through pull or bribes or threats or any sort of idolatry. That was bad news for the elect, the privileged, the professional holy men who thought they could select the kingdom. All of them were told by Jesus that they had to be elected to it.

While Jesus was talking, the chief priests and elders of Jerusalem met together in the palace of the High Priest, Caiaphas, and made plans to arrest Jesus secretly and put him to death. "We must not do it during the Feast," they said, "or the people will riot." Jesus had become a real danger to the establishment. It would no longer be just a luxury to kill him; it had become a political necessity. This Jesus had mocked and humiliated them in public, and now he was causing such a ruckus that he could at any time bring the Romans down on all of them. Getting rid of the troublemaker would be a cheap solution, and there were people close to Jesus who would be glad to help.

Just as Jesus had sensed might happen, Judas Iscariot, one of the twelve disciples, went to the chief priests and said, "What will you give me if I hand Jesus over to you?" The chief priests gave him thirty silver coins and from then on he looked for an opportunity to betray Jesus.

Jesus had gambled on Judas because he knew him to be a man of action and a sound administrator. Judas carried a dagger and also carried the purse of the group. The name Iscariot actually means "dagger carrier" and in Judas' case meant more than that. He was almost certainly a Zealot, a member of a paramilitary group dedicated to the overthrow of the Roman government in Palestine. His group had been seething and smoldering underground since the abortive revolt in 10 A.D. It was strange that he could be both a firebrand and an accountant. His administrative capacity hid a desperate soul which had first signed on with Jesus in fervent hope.

Judas had seen Jesus as a charismatic leader who could deliver the Jews. Discipleship had been, however, a terrible disappointment to Judas. Jesus had blown it. The Teacher had turned Galilee upside down and frenzied mobs screamed for him to be their king, and then he talked to them about the kingdom *within*. Within what? Right here on the outside was a God-given opportunity to take over and rule as King of the Jews—and smite the Romans with the edge of the sword. Jesus had everything going for him, in Judas' eyes. He was persuasive, he did miracles, he could lead. But he did not slaughter the enemy; he raised the dead. He did not call down pestilence on the Romans; he cured the sick. He did not multiply swords and spears; he multiplied fishes and loaves. He valued the meek and lowly, and disparaged the rich and the power' ful. Bitter frustration overwhelmed Judas when Jesus ran away and actually hid when they sought to make him king. So he took the thirty pieces of silver and promised to finger Jesus as soon as they could get him away from the crowds.

On the first day of the Feast of Unleavened Bread, some of his staff came to Jesus and asked where he wished to have the Passover supper. Jesus gave them instructions along with a cryptic message for a man in Jerusalem who was to provide the house. "Tell him," Jesus said, "that the Teacher says, 'My hour has come; my disciples and I will celebrate the Passover at your house.' " The staff fol' lowed his instructions, and the man said, "Fine," and they prepared the supper. During the meal, Jesus stared at them thoughtfully, almost fiercely, and said, "I tell you, one of you will betray me."

There was a tormentous awareness in Jesus that a mighty chain of onrushing events was already crashing down into darkness. There was almost no time left with his followers. When Jesus said at supper that one of them would betray him, they suddenly understood that he ex' pected it would happen very soon. There was enormous anxiety in the group and they began to ask him openly, "Surely you don't mean me, Lord?" "Is it I?" They were all lying on couches at right angles to the table and dipping

bread in the rich gravy, so Jesus looked around the table
and repeated his prediction: "One who dips his bread
in the dish with me will betray me. The Son of Man will
die as the scriptures say he will, but how terrible for that
man who will betray the Son of Man. It would have been
better for that man if he had never been born!"

Judas stood up. "Surely you don't mean me, Teacher?"
he asked. Jesus answered, "So you say." Then Jesus said
to him, "Hurry and do what you must." None of the
others understood this exchange, and since Judas was in
charge of the money they assumed that Jesus had sent
him to buy something else for the supper or to attend
to some other detail.

But Judas knew that Jesus knew, and he had braced him
with a question to be absolutely certain. As he left the
house and went into the city, Judas had an icy cramp
of emotion in his chest. He was obsessed with the tyranny
of Rome. Jesus was wrong and weak; he would not seize
his chance and go for the throat of Rome.

There was a final hated memory that Judas could not
keep out of his mind. Earlier that evening Jesus had taken
off his outer garments and had wrapped a towel around
his waist. Then he poured water into a basin and, to the
consternation and embarrassment of the disciples, he began
to wash their feet and dry them with a towel. Simon
Peter rebelled at this. "You will never at any time wash
my feet." "If I do not wash your feet," Jesus told him
very firmly, "you will no longer be my disciple." Simon
Peter said, "Lord, do not wash only my feet, then. Wash
my hands and head, too." When Jesus had finished, he
began to explain. "Do you understand what I have just

done to you? You call me Teacher and Lord, and it is
right that you should do so. I have just washed your feet.
You, then, should wash each other's feet." It was cus-
tomary for servants to wash feet in that time. Jesus had
brutally made his point that only out of humility could
man see the divine qualities in his fellow man, especially
if that fellow man were poor and helpless. This was more
than Judas could stand, and he could not bear to understand any of it.

With Judas gone, Jesus was more relaxed and talked
openly with the other disciples. "My children, I shall not
be with you very much longer. You will look for me, but
I tell you now what I told the Jews. 'You cannot go where
I am going.' A new commandment I give you: Love one
another. As I have loved you, so you must love one
another. If you have love for one another, then all will
know that you are my disciples."

While they were eating, Jesus took the bread, gave a
prayer of thanks, broke it, and gave it to his disciples.
"Take and eat it," he said, "this is my body." Then he
took the cup, gave thanks to God, and gave it to them.
"Drink it, all of you," he said; "for this is my blood, which
seals God's covenant, my blood poured out for many for
the forgiveness of sins. I tell you, I will never again drink
this wine until the day I drink it new with you in my
Father's Kingdom." Then they sang a hymn and went
out to the Mount of Olives.

"The disciples were at first mystified by the idea of the
bread being Jesus' body and the wine his blood. But
they were comforted by the ritual and the ideas began
to work inside of them and to strengthen them as if this

bread and this wine were great sources of strength from Jesus, that would continue to nourish them.

Jesus spoke very warmly and intimately to them as they sat in a sheltered place on the Mount of Olives. He even chided them as if they were children who would soon be on their own with no parents to counsel and guide them. "This very night," he said, "all of you will run away and leave me, for the scripture says, 'God will kill the shepherd and the sheep of the flock will be scattered.' But after I am raised to life I will go to Galilee ahead of you."

Peter would not accept that. "I will never leave you, even though all the rest do." "Remember this," Jesus sadly answered Peter. "Before the rooster crows tonight, you will say three times that you do not know me." Peter was insistent. He would never deny knowing Jesus even if he had to die for it, and all the other disciples said the same thing.

Then Jesus spoke encouraging words to them about preaching the good news. He reminded them that they had gone out on earlier field trips without any possessions and had been successful. "But now," Jesus said, "whoever has a purse or a bag must take it; and whoever does not have a sword must sell his coat and buy one." The disciples were excited and took account of things they had. "Look! here are two swords, Lord." "That is enough," he answered. Jesus was arming the disciples, literally and psychologically, for the campaigns ahead.

When the plans were made, Jesus looked at them with a great hollow aching that a parent feels inside when he looks at his children and knows he will not always be able to protect them.

"Let not your hearts be troubled, believe in God, be-lieve also in me," he said. "In my Father's house are many rooms; if it were not so, would I have told you that I go to prepare a place for you? And when I go and prepare a place for you, I will come again and will take you to myself, that where I am you may be also. And you know the way where I am going." This was too much for Thomas, and he said, "Lord, we do not know where you are going; how can we know the way?" Jesus said to him, "I am the way, and the truth, and the life; no one comes to the Father, but by me. If you had known me, you would have known my Father also; henceforth you know him and have seen him."

Jesus led the group to a place called Gethsemane where there was a garden. He asked them to sit there while he prayed. And he took Peter, James and John to be closer to him. Distress and anguish came over Jesus and he said to them, "My heart is so full of sorrow that I feel I may die. Stay here and watch." He went a little further and fell on the ground and prayed that, if possible, he might not have to go through this hour of suffering. "Father," he prayed, "my Father, all things are possible for you. Take this cup away from me. But not what I want, but what you want."

A second and a third time Jesus returned from praying by himself to find his companions asleep. They just could not keep their eyes open. The third time, as they sat there rubbing their eyes to hide their shame, he said, "Are you still sleeping and resting? Enough! The hour has come! Look, the Son of Man is now handed over to the power of sinful men. Here is the man who is betraying me."

Jesus had one instant of excitement and anxiety, and then the band he had been waiting for closed in on him. Judas led the way, followed by a group heavily armed with swords and clubs, and carrying torches.

"Teacher," said Judas as he stepped quickly up to Jesus and kissed him. As the others grabbed Jesus, Peter drew his sword and slashed at the man nearest him who had jumped forward. But Jesus said, "No more of this!" And he touched and healed the man whom Peter had slashed on the ear. For a moment Jesus was able to silence those who had surged forward to grab him. "Did you have to come with swords and clubs to capture me, as though I were an outlaw? Day after day I was with you teaching in the Temple, and you did not arrest me." His voice rang out over the heavy breathing as they bound him tightly. Then all of Jesus' followers scattered into the darkness. With one curious exception. A young man named Mark dressed only in a linen cloth did not run away with the others but doggedly stuck to Jesus. When they tried to arrest him also, he did break away and escaped naked, leaving the linen cloth behind.

The arresting party first led Jesus to Annas, a powerful shadowy figure who was the father-in-law of Caiaphas. It was Caiaphas who earlier advised his fellow Jews that it was better for one man to die than for all the people to suffer. He had offered this advice partly as prophecy and partly as practical political judgment, and now Jesus was being delivered to him.

Simon Peter and another disciple had followed Jesus and the guards at a distance. The other disciple was brave enough to go inside with the group that led Jesus to

Annas, but Peter waited outside by the gate. He felt lost and dismayed; he could not bear to let Jesus out of his sight, but he also dared not go closer. After awhile the other disciple came back to the gate and asked the girl there to let Peter inside. As he came in, the girl asked, "Aren't you one of the disciples of that man?" "No, I am not," Peter answered. It was cold at that hour of the night, and the servants and guards had built a charcoal fire and were standing around it warming themselves. Peter went over and stood with them.

In another room, Jesus was being questioned about his teaching and about the identity of his followers. He said, "I have spoken publicly to everyone; all my teaching was done in the meetinghouses and in the Temple, where all the Jews come together. I have never said anything in secret. Why then do you question me? Question the people who heard me. Ask them what I told them—they know what I said." One of the guards slapped Jesus in the face. "Is that how you answer a high priest?" Jesus kept his composure. "If I have said something wrong, tell everyone here what it was. But, if I am right in what I have said, why do you hit me?"

Annas sent him, still bound, to Caiaphas, the High Priest. This had been a standard interrogation, but Jesus' answers were disquietingly open and believable. The priests, and especially the guards, knew by the rhythm and ring of his voice that Jesus did not seem to be either frightened or guilty. Once the legal process had started, however, Jesus was moved along with that sure competence the law shows in accomplishing its own end.

Now thoroughly miserable and frightened, Simon Peter

was standing with the guards around the fire. And one of the guards who had been watching him for some time in the heightening light, challenged him: "Aren't you one of the disciples of that man?" "No, man, I am not," Peter said in his unmistakably Galilean accent. As the man was about to retort, a kinsman of the guard that Peter had slashed with his sword joined the group. "Didn't I see you with him in the garden?" he asked. "No," Peter said frantically. It was near dawn and at once a rooster crowed. Peter remembered that Jesus had said to him, "Before the cock crows twice, you will deny me three times." And he went out and wept bitterly.

As soon as it was fully light the whole company took Jesus from the house of Caiaphas to the Governor's palace. The Jews would not go into the palace of the gentile governor because they wanted to keep themselves ritually clean for the Passover meal. When Pontius Pilate, Governor of Judea, was told that a band of Jews from the High Court had come with a prisoner, the notorious Jesus of Nazareth, he came out with considerable interest to meet the party.

Jesus was being railroaded into the hands of the authority that could impose the death penalty for political crimes. But this was exactly the sort of sticky situation that Pilate wanted to avoid. He was a treacherous, willful man, but he was cunning enough to see the danger of taking sides in the superheated disputes of the Jews. Besides, it was still early and Pilate felt as if he had been cooked in wine the night before. He pulled himself together with the strength that all successful politicians can muster when they have to, and said, "Yes, what can I do for you?"

The Jews silently thrust Jesus forward. "What do you accuse this man of?" Pilate asked. A spokesman for the Temple officials said, "We would not have brought him to you if he had not committed a crime."

"You take him yourselves and try him according to your own law," Pilate said forcefully, hoping he could get this hairy problem back into the hands of the Jews. "We can't—we are not allowed to put anyone to death," the Jews said. And then Pilate knew what he feared was true, that he was being used. "We found this man subvert-ing our nation," they said. "He was opposing the payment of taxes to Caesar and claiming to be a Messiah, a king."

Pilate motioned to the Roman guards, who took Jesus in hand, and they went back into the palace where they could talk privately, while the Jewish officials waited out-side. "Are you king of the Jews?" Pilate asked. Jesus asked, "Does this question come from you or have others told you about me?" "Do you think I am a Jew?" Pilate snorted. "It was your own people and their chief priests who handed you over to me. What have you done?"

Speaking to the point of the charge by the Jews, Jesus replied, "My kingdom does not belong to this world; if my kingdom belonged to this world, my followers would fight to keep me from being handed over to the Jews. No, my kingdom does not belong here."

Pilate demanded, "Are you a king, then?" "You say that I am a king," Jesus said. "I was born and came into the world for this one purpose, to speak about the truth.

Whoever belongs to the truth listens to me." "And what is truth?" Pilate asked. Jesus didn't answer. He was not interested in getting into a debate with Pilate. He did speak for the record to make it incontrovertibly clear that he was not a revolutionary advocating the overthrow of Rome. As he told the priests earlier that same morning, "I have never said anything in secret." And now Jesus was telling Pilate in a different way that the kingdom he was organizing had nothing to do with the rule of Rome.

To speak the truth was Jesus' whole story—it was the the good news. Pilate listened. But Jesus didn't try to make a shoestring conversion of Pilate to save himself. He never tried to convert anybody to save himself, or even to help himself. As for Pilate's question "What is truth?" Jesus had already answered that for his own followers. He had said to Thomas, "I am the way, and the truth, and the life: no man comes unto the Father but by me." And on another occasion he said to an audience, "If you obey my teachings you are really my disciples; you will know the truth and the truth will make you free." In that moment of interrogation, the only truth that Jesus was about to tell Pilate was that he, Jesus of Nazareth, was not a Zealot, and that the Jews were trying to satisfy a blood lust by political means that were not sanctified by either their Law or Pilate's.

Pilate sensed that he didn't have a Zealot on his hands, but he was juggling a hot coal. So he went back outside to the Temple officials and told them he could find no reason to condemn Jesus. They were not pleased. They upped the charges. "He is starting a riot among the people with his teaching! He began in Galilee, went through all of Judea, and now he has come here." Pilate's mind suddenly clicked—he found the out that he had been searching for. "Is this man a Galilean?" he asked. And when they said yes, he was immensely relieved, because that region was ruled by Herod, who happened to be in Jerusalem at that time.

Pontius Pilate summarily sent Jesus off to Herod, and went back to bed. Herod Antipas was delighted to hear that Jesus was being brought to his court. He had heard many stories of Jesus' Galilean ministry and had been especially fascinated by the reports of his miracles. Having grown up in a tempestuous home under the influence of a tyrannical father, Herod was enormously self-indulgent, and nothing diverted him so much as magic. He thought it very generous of Pilate to send Jesus along to amuse him.

Judas had followed the action after Jesus' arrest. When he saw Jesus being led from Pilate's palace to Herod's office in the little jurisdictional game that had to end in Jesus' destruction, he was horrified with what he had done. His bitter enemies, the Romans, had Jesus in their hands. Somehow this changed everything. If he had despaired of Jesus and been contemptuous of his failure to rally men to revolt, then he had been betrayed by his own fury when he delivered his teacher to the Jews. For the Jews had delivered him in turn to the Romans. The larger consequences bore in on Judas: he had betrayed an innocent man and turned him over as a victim to vassals and tyrants.

Wholly desperate, Judas returned to the elders who had paid him the silver coins. "I have sinned by betraying an innocent man to death!" he said. "What do we care about that?" they said contemptuously. "That is your business." So Judas threw the money into the sanctuary, ran out, and hanged himself. The elders retrieved the money but they hesitated to put it in their Temple treasury because it was technically blood money. Ever worshipfully attentive to the letter of the Law, they decided that the appropriate thing to do with the silver coins would be to buy land for a cemetery for foreigners. It is called the "Field of Blood" to this day.

Herod, in the meantime, had settled down to be enter- tained by Jesus. It did not go well. Herod questioned him about the wonders he had performed, and peremp- torily demanded a sign or miracle. Jesus did not answer a word. The priests and lawyers stepped forward and made strong accusations against Jesus. And then Herod used Jesus for sport, and he and his soldiers mocked and treated him with contempt. Finally, they put a rich robe on Jesus and sent him back to Pilate. It is said that on that very day Herod and Pilate, who had been enemies before, became friends.

Jerusalem was filling up by this time with pilgrims gathering for the Passover Feast; and here was Jesus back again with Pilate—Herod had unloaded him. Pilate had one more scheme for getting off the hook. Remembering one Passover custom that might work to his advantage, he called together the Jewish leaders and reviewed what had happened. "You brought this man to me and said that he was misleading the people," Pilate said. "Now, I have examined him here in your presence and I have not found him guilty of any of the bad things you accuse him of.

Nor did Herod find him guilty, for he sent him back to us. There is nothing this man has done to deserve death. I will have him whipped, then, and let him go." Pilate said this knowing that each Passover Feast it was the custom to free one condemned prisoner as the Roman contribution to the occasion. If he could set Jesus free his problem would be solved.

But the priests and lawyers fanned out through the crowd and sent other messengers to spread the word and stir the people up. "Kill Jesus! Shout 'Kill Jesus!' " they told the people. "Ask that Barabbas be set free," they whispered. Barabbas was a notorious Zealot who had been imprisoned for inciting a riot in the city and for murder. Pilate wanted to set Jesus free because he was struck by the innocence of Jesus, and he knew Barabbas was a fanatical and dangerous enemy of Rome. Soon voices in the crowd were crying out for the death of Jesus, and then the whole crowd was screaming, "Kill him! Kill him! Set Barabbas free for us!"

Pilate exhorted the crowd to let Jesus go. In a curiously contradictory posture for him, he almost pled with the crowd. "But what crime has he committed? I cannot find anything he has done to deserve death. I will have him whipped and set him free." The irony of this situation was that an unsavory procurator was trying to save a man accused by the High Court of subverting the country and disrupting the collection of taxes by Rome.

A bad governor who had gone out of his way to offend the Jews, in violation of the political wisdom and practice of Rome, Pilate had suddenly become emotionally in-volved in the fate of Jesus. He wasn't daunted by the thought of crucifixion itself—having people crucified was almost a daily routine for Pilate. Like most Romans of the time, if he didn't positively enjoy torture, he at least took it as a matter of course. Jesus had gotten to Pilate. But whatever deep instinct he had for saving Jesus was finally overwhelmed by the shouts of the crowd.

The roar was deafening. It was a wild, rolling refrain of "Nail him to the cross! Nail him to the cross!" Pilate could see tossing angry movements that told his practiced eye that a riot was building at that moment. When he saw that it was no use to go on, that the situation would be out of control at any second, he had a basin of water brought to him and he washed his hands in front of the crowd. "I am not responsible for the death of this man," he told the mob. "This is your doing." They screamed back at him, "Let the punishment for his death fall on us and on our children."

Then Pilate set Barabbas free; and he had Jesus whipped and handed over to be nailed to the cross. With the help of the mob, the Jewish establishment had accomplished what they set out to do many months before. In a brilliant tactical move they had given the people a choice between Jesus and Barabbas. Of course the Pharisees and the priests did not have any use for Barabbas, they were scared to death of him; but in the short term he wasn't as dangerous to them as Jesus. And the common people, excited by the fire of the Zealots, were crawling with hostility for Rome and hungry for ways of expressing it.

They didn't understand that Jesus was fighting for the overthrow of the evil in man. The terms of this battle were different. Winning it depends on a much higher

passion; it depends on stirring the passion of love. As
Jesus learned, many are eager to enlist if you will lead
them with hate to overthrow with might.

Pilate's soldiers took Jesus into the Governor's palace,
and the whole company gathered around him. They
stripped off his clothes and put a scarlet robe on him.
Then they made a crown out of thorn branches and put
it on his head, and they stuck a reed in his right hand.
"Long live the King of the Jews!" they said as they knelt
before him and made fun of him. They spat upon him
and took a stick and hit him over the head with it. When
they had tired of their sport, they put his own clothes
back on him and led him out to nail him to the cross.

The soldiers forced Jesus to carry his cross on his back.
Weak from the whippings, he toiled out of the gates of
the city and up toward the hill of Golgotha which had
been appointed as the place of execution. The Romans
used whips of many tails with pieces of metal tied into the
ends of the thongs, so that Jesus was now gashed and
bleeding over all of his body from the beatings. The
soldiers could see that Jesus was breaking under the
weight of the cross and they wanted to save him for
the crucifixion. So they seized a hapless passerby, Simon of
Cyrene, who was coming in from the country, and they
forced him to carry the cross.

A large crowd swarmed along after Jesus and the soldiers. Most of them were the same sort who have gone
to executions throughout history as free entertainment.
But many who trailed along were desolate. Among the
grievers were some women who wept and wailed. Jesus
turned to them and said, "Women of Jerusalem. Don't

cry for me but for yourselves and your children. The days are coming when people will say, 'How lucky are the women who never had children, who never bore babies, who never nursed them!' That will be the time when people will say to the mountains, 'Fall on us!' and to the hills, 'Hide us!' For if such things as this are done when the wood is green, what will it be like when it is dry?"

Entirely human and caught in a brutally dehumanizing ordeal, Jesus was still aware of those around him, and he had responded to the ladies. Tears may have been more than he could stand at the moment.

When they got to the top of the hill, the soldiers perfunctorily offered Jesus the ritual drink of wine mixed with myrrh to ease the pain of crucifixion. Jesus turned it down—probably so that he would have more control over the way he behaved on the cross. Then they threw Jesus down and pinioned his arms. A Roman soldier put his knee on Jesus' elbow and threw the whole weight of his body on it. The forearm was now paralyzed. They drove a spike through that hand with a huge wooden mallet. Then they nailed down the other hand the same way. And they immobilized his knees and drove a spike through his feet. With brute strength they savaged the cross up, and as they blocked it forward, it lugged into its socket with a jolt; the body sagged down on the nails, tearing the muscles and twisting the spinal column. This tearing wrench caused blood and body fluid to spurt out; it was the greatest loss of blood during the crucifixion.

When Jesus' full weight hung on the nails, he writhed in agony, and he said, "Father, forgive them; for they know not what they do."

Then the soldiers crucified two bandits, one on Jesus'

right and one on his left. Once the dirty work was done, the soldiers moved back to rest and watch. The way was clear and the high priests stepped forward in front of Jesus. "Aha!" they said, wagging their heads. "You were going to tear down the Temple and build it up in three days. Now come down from the cross and save yourself. Let us see the Messiah, the King, come down from the cross now and we will believe in him."

Many of these tormentors with the hard minds and the stout stomachs were religious leaders of Jerusalem, but others were strangers who couldn't turn down the opportunity of piling on abuse. Not all insulted Jesus or ridiculed him. One criminal attacked him and begged him, "Aren't you the Messiah? Save yourself and us!" The other bandit broke in. "Don't you fear God? Here we all are under the same sentence. Ours is only right, for we are getting what we deserve for what we did; but he has done no wrong." And he said to Jesus, "Remember me, Jesus, when you come as king." Jesus said to him, "I tell you this: today you will be in Paradise with me."

Just as Jesus had had the temerity to associate with every kind of sinner, he had the fate to be crucified with a bandit on either side of him. He never took his eyes off the lost sheep. The devout members of the ruling group, whom he had never liked nearly so well as the sinners, watched him with still, incurious eyes. And other casual folks out for the day stood by while the crucifixion was going on just on the chance that they might see Elijah come down to set him free, or to see God take Jesus from the cross.

Of those that loved Jesus, the women had the courage

and devotion to stand closest to the cross. There at the foot of the cross were Jesus' mother, his mother's sister, Mary the wife of Cleopas, and Mary Magdalene. But next to Jesus' mother stood a disciple whom Jesus especially loved. Jesus looked at the two of them, and said to his mother, "Woman, here is your son." Then he said to the disciple, "Here is your mother." And from that time the disciple took her to live in his home.

At noon a darkness began to cover the whole countryside. It caught the full attention of the onlookers and fanned the spark of suspicion that more than just another rebel had been crucified. At the third hour of his crucifixion, Jesus cried out, "My God, my God, why did you abandon me?" Some of the bystanders thought he was calling for Elijah. One of them ran up with a sponge, soaked it in a bowl of cheap wine, and put it on the end of a stick. Then he held it up to Jesus' lips and said, "Wait. Let us see if Elijah is coming to bring him down from the cross." But Jesus cried out with another shout, "Father, into thy hands I commit my spirit!"

The light of the sun failed and the curtain of the Temple of Jerusalem was torn in two from top to bottom. A Roman centurion who was at the scene of the crucifixion was overcome and praised God, saying, "Certainly he was a good man." The woman and the disciples and the friends of Jesus didn't notice that the sky was dark. For them, another light was out. This life that had lit the fires on a thousand hills was ended. That so large a soul, that a man so full of life, could be taken away as one cry faded to silence, shattered them. All of this made such a loneliness in the hearts of those who knew him that they could not breathe. Jesus was gone.

〖 EPILOGUE 〗

ON THE Sunday after Jesus' death two men were walking from Jerusalem to Emmaus, a seven-mile hike. Followers of the Teacher, they were still stunned and bitter about the terrible events of the past days. And they were further confused and distraught over the wild reports of Mary Magdalene and Joanna and Mary the mother of James; these women claimed to have met and talked with angels that very morning who announced that Jesus was alive.

They were talking about the things that had happened in the last few days, when Jesus overtook them and joined them. Cleopas and his companion did not recognize Jesus, so he asked them what they had been talking about and why they looked sad. They told him how the mighty prophet, Jesus of Nazareth, had been delivered up by the high priests to be condemned to death and crucified by the Romans. "It is now the third day since this happened," Cleopas said, "and some women of our company gave us amazing news this morning. They went to his tomb early in the morning and did not find his body, but instead they saw a vision of angels who said that he was alive. Some of our group went to the grave and found it exactly as the women had said but they did not see him."

Then Jesus said to them, "How foolish you are, how slow you are to believe everything the prophets said. Was it not necessary for the Messiah to suffer these things and to enter his glory?" And then he explained to them what was said about him in all the scriptures, beginning with the books of Moses and the writings of all the prophets.

They urged the stranger to stay the night with them in a village on the way, and when he said the blessing and broke the bread, they recognized him. Then Jesus disappeared from their sight. One of the men said, "Wasn't it like a fire burning in us when he talked to us on the road and explained the scriptures?"

71 72 73 10 9 8 7 6 5 4 3 2 1